Managing Diversity

Roger Cartwright

- ■ *The* fast track route to mastering all aspects of managing a diverse workforce

- ■ Covers all the key techniques for managing diversity successfully, from motivating all parts of the workforce to techniques for avoiding stereotyping, and from managing the multilingual organization to using technology

- ■ Examples and lessons from some of the world's most successful businesses, including Coca Cola, British Airways and Mitsubishi, and ideas from the smartest thinkers, including Richard Lewis and Fons Trompenaars

- ■ Includes a glossary of key concepts and a comprehensive resources guide

PEOPLE

09.06

>>EXPRESS EXEC.COM<<

essential management thinking at your fingertips

First published 2002 by
Capstone Publishing (A Wiley Company)
8 Newtec Place
Magdalen Road
Oxford OX4 1RE
United Kingdom
http://www.capstoneideas.com

CIP catalogue records for this book are available from the British Library and the US Library of Congress

ISBN 1-84112-246-7

Printed and bound in Great Britain

This book is printed on acid-free paper

Substantial discounts on bulk quantities of Capstone books are available to corporations, professional associations and other organizations. Please contact Capstone for more details on +44 (0)1865 798 623 or (fax) +44 (0)1865 240 941 or (e-mail) info@wiley-capstone.co.uk

Contents

Introduction to ExpressExec   v

09.06.01 Introduction to Managing Diversity   1
09.06.02 What is Managing Diversity?   5
09.06.03 The Evolution of Managing Diversity   11
09.06.04 The E-Dimension in Managing Diversity   21
09.06.05 The Global Dimension of Managing Diversity   31
09.06.06 The State of the Art of Managing Diversity   41
09.06.07 Managing Diversity Success Stories   59
09.06.08 Key Concepts and Thinkers in Managing
          Diversity   79
09.06.09 Resources for Managing Diversity   93
09.06.10 Ten Steps to Making Managing Diversity work   101

Frequently Asked Questions (FAQs)   109
Index   113

Introduction to ExpressExec

ExpressExec is 3 million words of the latest management thinking compiled into 10 modules. Each module contains 10 individual titles forming a comprehensive resource of current business practice written by leading practitioners in their field. From brand management to balanced scorecard, ExpressExec enables you to grasp the key concepts behind each subject and implement the theory immediately. Each of the 100 titles is available in print and electronic formats.

Through the ExpressExec.com Website you will discover that you can access the complete resource in a number of ways:

» printed books or e-books;
» e-content – PDF or XML (for licensed syndication) adding value to an intranet or Internet site;
» a corporate e-learning/knowledge management solution providing a cost-effective platform for developing skills and sharing knowledge within an organization;
» bespoke delivery – tailored solutions to solve your need.

Why not visit www.expressexec.com and register for free key management briefings, a monthly newsletter and interactive skills checklists. Share your ideas about ExpressExec and your thoughts about business today.

Please contact elound@wiley-capstone.co.uk for more information.

Introduction to Managing Diversity

This introduction to managing diversity stresses the benefits to organizations of making the fullest use of the skills and experience of the diversity of staff that can often be found in even small organizations. This theme will be expanded throughout this material.

"If we cannot now end our differences, at least we can help make the world safe for diversity."

John F. Kennedy, 1963

With the exception of identical twins, no two humans are exactly alike. The double helix of DNA (deoxyribonucleic acid), with its four building blocks, contains sufficient combinations to make each and every individual who has ever lived (unless he or she is the result of multiple births from the same egg) different from everybody else; thus diversity is in our very nature.

People are the most precious resource that any organization has. Whilst computers can perform many routine and intricate tasks better than humans, they lack the ability to be creative and to project into the future. The also lack the ability to sympathize and empathize with others and to apologize, and these are the type of relationship skills that are so important when motivating others or dealing with customers.

When account is taken of suppliers, employees, customers, and other stakeholders, even the smallest organization deals with a large number of people. In even the most closed economy these are likely to consist of males and females of differing ages and abilities. In the modern global economy, those managing organizations may be working with people whose culture, practices and language are far different to their own. Whilst diversity can present problems, although never ones that cannot be overcome, it can also provide wonderful opportunities.

It was only at the end of the twentieth century that humankind began to realize the importance of preserving biodiversity on the earth. In managerial and organizational terms, diversity presents the opportunity provided by new skills and ideas as well as the opening up of new markets. Diversity, however, also requires a change in managerial practices: all people cannot be treated as though they were the same. Even within a small, fairly homogenous group there will be different personalities and aspirations within the members and this means that they will be motivated by different factors.

Researchers such as Meredith Belbin in the UK, whose work will feature later in this book, have shown how successful workplace groups are composed of different personalities working in what might be described as harmonic tension. They have the tensions that exist between people who react and behave differently because of their diverse personalities, but who are able to harness their differences to act in a relationship of synergy which can hold a group together in harmony and produce better results than might be expected if each member were considered purely as an individual.

Modern managers are likely to find themselves working not only with those of different ages, genders and work experience, but also with those who have had different educational opportunities, who come from a different part of the world, who have a different culture, and who speak a different language. Harnessing the potential of such diversity requires a reappraisal of managerial skills. It also requires, as a first step, a realization that nobody is better than anybody else, whether judgements are based on where people come from, the language they speak or the values they hold. They may be different, but that does not imply that they are better or worse – either in the workplace or in society in general: they are different, and they are part of the diversity that can make organizations more productive.

What is Managing Diversity?

» In essence, managing diversity is about using all of the talents available to the organization without resorting to ethnocentricity and stereotyping.

» Managing diversity sounds easy in theory but in practice our prejudices may be part of our cultural upbringing and it may take considerable effort, and even soul-searching, to free ourselves from them. The rewards, however, are well worth the effort.

» By understanding each worker and where he or she is coming from, a manager can select the right motivators for that person and thus produce the best results.

The quote from President Kennedy that began this book implies that difference and diversity, whilst related, are not synonymous. *Difference* is a very precise term, something is either different or it is the same. *Diversity* is much broader; things can be diverse but still similar. Diverse implies a range, blending one into another rather like the colors in a spectrum of light change from infra red through the visible colors across to ultra-violet.

As will be pointed out in Chapter 3, it is a paradox that whilst the world has been made smaller through technology, its diversity has become more apparent. For the world of work this diversity is now manifested in a much less homogenous work force that, in turn, requires new management ideas in order to use that diversity to its best advantage.

Human beings, wherever they come from, share certain basic attributes, not least of which is that they belong to a single species – *Homo sapiens*. One way of telling whether individuals belong to the same species is their ability to produce young that are not sterile. Closely related species can breed but produce offspring suffering from sterility. Thus a donkey and a horse (closely related species) can breed but the offspring – a mule – will be sterile.

As animals, human beings are primates. Physically, primates have evolved with three very important characteristics that have also had a major effect on their behavioral evolution. The first is stereoscopic vision, important for our ancestors who began life swinging from branch to branch and thus needed to gauge distance very accurately. The second is color vision – many primates are fruit eaters and fruits tend to be brightly colored. The third, of critical importance, is the way our hands, wrists and arms are connected. Primates are able to touch their thumb to all fingers (known as *opposition*) and are able to rotate the two bones in the lower arm, the radius and the ulna, over each other. This provides us with an extremely complex joint and movement system which is ideal not only for twisting fruit off branches but also for the manipulation of tools. Humans have also evolved to walk upright, thus freeing the hand and arms to manipulate tools without the need to put them down in order to move from place to place.

Primates are group animals, and as such have developed complex visual and aural communications systems. They are not alone in this;

bees have a very sophisticated visual communications system using dance to point out the direction to a food supply, and the whale family is known to have a considerable language repertoire. However, no other species has the language ability of humans.

Unfortunately one of the drawbacks of being a primate in the modern world is that our psychological evolution, a term coined by Nigel Nicholson in his book *Managing the Human Animal* (2000), appears to be still in the Stone Age. As group animals we value our membership and we try to exclude non-group members from sharing our resources and territory. Perhaps like gorillas, baboons and chimpanzees we are still locked into a tribal culture. Our technological ability, however, has produced working and living patterns that throw members of different groups together with increasing regularity. It is possible that our future evolution will not be physical but psychological and social.

Living creatures have evolved in response to changes in the external, natural environment. Humans are able to manipulate the external environment to a degree unprecedented in the past, a trend that is likely to accelerate. We are still unable to prevent earthquakes and other natural phenomena, but increasingly we can minimize the effects of the natural world. We are still caught out, as global warming has shown, and it may be some time before we have any defense against a large meteor from space, but more and more we are adapting the environment to suit ourselves. Whether in doing so we shall actually destroy the very planet we live on is a point of increasing discussion.

Most human conflict has been about preventing those who are different from acquiring resources. In this situation, the tribal instinct seems to be very powerful. In the 1930s, the German government encouraged some of the world's greatest scientists to emigrate because they did not fit the racial stereotype that Adolf Hitler demanded for the country. Imagine the way history might read if Albert Einstein had continued working in Germany and Hitler had acquired nuclear weapons before the allies! To support a racial principle, Hitler was prepared to see such talent leave Germany to assist others.

Whilst the physical differences between humans may be relatively easy to distinguish – age, gender, skin pigmentation, etc. – the intrinsic differences between groups are to be found at the cultural level. Culture, as described by Fons Trompenaars the distinguished Dutch author of

Riding the Waves of Culture (1993), is the way in which a group of people solve problems; in essence, 'the way we do things around here'. Culture is made up of a set of values, attitudes and beliefs that differ from one culture to another. The more closely related one group is with another, the more cultural overlap there is likely to be between their cultures. This can explain the special relationship between the US and the UK, as the cultural roots of many (but not all) Americans are very similar to indigenous citizens of the UK. Huntingdon, writing in 1996 stated that "... the fundamental source of human conflict in this new world will not be primarily ideological or primarily economic. The great divisions among humankind and the dominating source of conflict will be culture." (*The Clash of Civilizations and the Remaking of World Order*, 1996). Whilst world conflict is a task for politicians to solve, the globalization of business means that managers will be working with diverse cultures and that maximum results are likely to come from a harnessing of all of the available talents.

One of the dangers of believing that one's own culture is better than any other, i.e. an ethnocentric approach, apart from the fact that the ultimate result leads to genocide, is a failure to utilize the full resources available. No one culture has ever had a monopoly on being right. In the western world alone we use paper money invented by the Chinese, mathematics developed in an Arab culture, a system of justice that has its roots with the Romans, and a way of thinking that began in ancient Greece. In addition many profess a religious belief, whether Jewish, Christian or Muslim, that began over two thousand years ago in the Middle East. This is a diversity that humankind has been able to manage.

Cultural beliefs are very deeply held and are passed down from generation to generation. Unfortunately prejudices are also passed on this way. Nothing stands more solidly in the way of managing diversity and obtaining the best results than the manager's prejudices about the worker and the worker's prejudices about his or her manager.

Up to the industrial revolution, few people had traveled much beyond their birthplace. Organizations were small and the workforce tended to be homogenous, with similar backgrounds and a similar culture. The management of cultural diversity was not an issue. After the large-scale population movements of the nineteenth and early twentieth centuries (as described in the next chapter) this was no longer the case.

F. W. Taylor, the originator of the concept of scientific management, was appointed as a management consultant at the Bethlehem Steel Corporation in 1898. He proceeded to conduct a series of management experiments on a workforce that was extremely diverse and contained not only those born in the US but those who had arrived from nearly every western and eastern European country, all with their own cultures and their own languages. The results of these experiments led to ideas of scientific management, piecework and a very structured work pattern based solely on pay as a motivator.

It is not only the US that has developed a diverse workforce. The UK has received many immigrants from Commonwealth countries. France has a large North African and Indo-Chinese workforce as a result of previous colonial activities, and Germany is host to a *Gästarbeiter* (guestworker) population from Turkey and other Balkan areas. All these people bring in their skills – but also their culture, and thus management techniques that could be applied to a homogenous workforce may be less applicable. The aim of managers should be to "advance diversity rather than adversity," a saying ascribed to Ken Chenault, who was appointed president and COO of American Express in 1997 and thus became the highest ranking African-American in the US business world.

On the micro-level there will be differences in personality between employees, just as there are gender differences at work between men and women (an issue to be covered later). The UK researcher Dr Meredith Belbin has produced a theory of team roles based on personality types and designed to allow managers to obtain the best results from groupings of diverse personalities (*see* Chapter 6).

The third major type of diversity has developed as owners and managers of organizations have realized, either through common sense or in reaction to legislation, that disability may be no reason for denying a qualified person employment. One need only consider the case of Stephen Hawking, the UK physicist and author of *A Brief History of Time*, to see that in his case at least, being wheelchair-bound through disease has been no bar to a brilliant intellect that has brought understanding of issues of time and space to millions worldwide through his writing and his work as an academic. Both the US, through the Americans with Disabilities Act, and the UK, with its Disabled Persons (Employment) Acts, have sought to ensure that those with disabilities who wish to work are enabled to do so. However, legislation can only go so far, and at last employers are realizing that talent should not be wasted and that a few small adaptations to the design of offices and workplaces can enable a first-class mind to be brought in and that it can do just as good a job as somebody without a disability.

KEY LEARNING POINTS

» Human beings are primates and this is the source of our physical structure and behavioral evolution.

» Humans are psychologically and socially adapted for living in a group situation.

» Human societies develop their own cultures, i.e. a distinct set of values, attitudes, and beliefs.

» There is a danger of ethnocentricity – believing that one's own culture and way of doing things are superior to those of others.

» Modern transportation has changed the situation whereby the vast majority of workgroups were homogenous – today's workforce may consist of individuals from diverse backgrounds and cultures.

» Even within a relatively homogenous workforce there will be individual personality differences leading to another form of diversity for managers to deal with.

» Those with disabilities may be just as valuable and productive employees as those without disabilities.

The Evolution of Managing Diversity

» The world has become a much smaller place in the twentieth century as the speeds of communications and transportation increased dramatically. Steamships and railways allowed for mass emigration especially from Europe to North America, with over 12 million people leaving Europe for the US between 1892 and 1924.

» Towns and cities have also grown, with their populations spreading out from the center. Transportation systems have meant that workers no longer need to live near to their place of work, which provides more choice for the employees and a more diverse workforce for the employer.

» The early work on scientific management by Taylor in the late 1890s proposed a very mechanistic management style that treated all workers on an equal basis, with motivation based purely on financial incentive. Current thinking suggests that different motivational factors affect different people at varying stages of their careers, and that diverse styles of management contingent upon particular situations may be more effective.

» Equity is a more useful concept than equality, implying fairness.

The world of the early twenty-first century is very different from that of 1900 – and almost unrecognizable from conditions in 1800. Much of the difference is directly attributable to technology – and particularly to the vast increase in the speed of communications. In 1800, the fastest a message could travel beyond the line of sight was about 15–20 mph (24–32 kph); the speed of a person on horseback. The invention of the telegraph in the second half of the nineteenth century meant that a message could travel at the speed of an electric current, which is the same as the speed of light – approximately 186,000 miles per *second* (298,000 kilometers per second). That was a massive increase for messages, but the speed of transporting people was increasing too, as was the number of people that could be transported at any one time. The railways rapidly increased speeds from 20 mph in the early days up to 60 mph, and eventually 100 mph, which was achieved on the Great Western Railway in the UK in 1904. Whereas a stagecoach could carry eight to twelve passengers, an express train could move hundreds far more quickly and in much greater safety.

The effect of the railways on both Europe and North America was dramatic. The first passenger railway operated by steam locomotives running to a fixed timetable was between Liverpool and Manchester in the UK and was opened in 1830: the Baltimore and Ohio Railway in the US began operating later that same year. By 1850 there were 7500 miles of railroad in the US and on May 10, 1869, when the Union Pacific and the Central Pacific lines met at Promontory Summit, Utah; the rails now stretched across the US from the East to the West Coasts. The stage was set for a massive movement of human beings, encouraged by offers of land alongside the railroads as the US government sought to open up the lands west of the Mississippi. By 1888 the extent of railroad track in the US had grown to 156,082 miles, with a number of transcontinental lines in operation. In Canada, too, the railroads had opened up huge tracts of land, and there was hardly a town in Europe without a rail connection.

The same steam power that had revolutionized land transport also led to a huge increase in the size and speed of ships, especially on the North Atlantic between North America and Europe. The first regular steam passenger service on the North Atlantic run was that of the Canadian entrepreneur, Samuel Cunard, whose steamers commenced operations in 1840 and carried 63 passengers – and the all-important UK Royal Mail, whose subsidy made the operation possible. In 1840 the voyage took 11 days; by 1900 it was completed in less than a week. The largest passenger ship in existence in 1901, White Star Line's 20,904 grt (gross registered tonnage) *Celtic*, carried 2857 passengers, 2350 of whom were in the steerage accommodation usually used by emigrants. Even the *Celtic* was dwarfed by the Cunard vessels *Mauritania* and *Lusitania* of 1906, the *Olympic* of 1911, the ill-fated *Titanic* of 1912, and a series of large German liners that took the size over 50,000 grt, and the capacity to 3909, in the *Vaterland* of 1914 (a vessel later to become the US registered *Leviathan* after the end of World War I).

Mass emigration brought about by war and famine in Europe had become big business for the ship owners and provided the growing United States with a much-needed source of labor. Immigrants arrived at east and west coast ports; many Chinese and Japanese workers arrived in California from the 1860s onwards to work on the railroad construction gangs. On the east coast, the European immigrants began to fan out all over the country. The immigrant reception center on Ellis Island in New York Harbor is now a museum and provides a graphic display of how America grew with the aid of these immigrants, who arrived at precisely the right time to assist in the massive industrialization that occurred after the end of the US Civil War in 1865.

This massive immigration not only boosted American industry, it also gave the US a diversity that no other countries had previously experienced. Migration of peoples has been a constant human phenomenon but never in the numbers that entered the US. Between 1892 and 1924, when US immigration laws became much stricter, it is calculated that over 12 million immigrants arrived at Ellis Island; 1.5 million in a single year – 1913. Of these, all but 250,000 were allowed to enter the US. A very small percentage did eventually return to their original homes, but the vast majority stayed and raised families, and in time became 'American' – citizens of a nation that is perhaps the most diverse ever seen. It is true that the former Soviet Union also contained a large number of nationalities, but many of these were subjugated through armed conflict. The majority of those who formed the US we know today (apart from descendants of slaves and Native Americans) did so voluntarily.

SUBURBAN AND SUB-DIVISION DEVELOPMENT

In addition to contributing to the process of human migration and dispersal, the railroads and streetcars (trams as they are known in Europe) had a very important effect on a more local scale on the nature of organizations. Prior to their introduction, workers had no choice but to live in close proximity to their workplace. Hours were long, and energy and time could not be wasted on walking long distances. The size and location of factories and other employment sources was in danger of becoming limited by the need for them to be surrounded by low-cost housing for the workforce. Rail-borne transport, and its rival and later successor the bus, allowed large numbers of workers to live at increasingly greater distances from their places of employment. This in turn provided employees with more opportunities with different employers, and so employers developed a more diverse workforce.

Today, many organizations prefer to operate on the outskirts of population centers, but during the industrial revolution it was the more central areas of towns and cities that saw the development of factories and warehouses. This produced concentric circles of activities, with the municipal offices in the very center, then retail activities, followed by manufacturing and workers' accommodation, then the suburbs, and finally the rural areas – all linked by an increasingly efficient urban rail or streetcar network. It was this network that enabled employees to move further and further away from the noise and grime of the workplace, and led to the development of blue- and white-collar suburbs and sub-divisions that are still recognizable today. It also removed the stranglehold that company housing had on people: they could now move jobs without losing their home, which would be rented from a private landlord and not the company. Interestingly, the pattern of movement outwards from the city center to the suburbs is now being reversed, with the gentrification of many inner-city areas and the conversion of former industrial buildings to provide housing for the more affluent.

In the late 1890s, when F. W. Taylor (*see* Chapter 2) began to compile his ideas on scientific management, employers believed that all workers could be treated the same and that the common motivator was money. It must be remembered that slavery was still a very real memory for many at this time, as the UK had only abolished slavery in its colonies in 1833 and the US at the end of the Civil War in

1865. Indeed, there are parts of the world where slavery still exists today, despite the efforts of the United Nations and other international agencies to stamp out the trade. Slaves are not paid, and motivation for them was probably based on the avoidance of pain and hunger rather than on the acquisition of money.

MOTIVATION OF THE WORKFORCE

The idea that money was the prime motivator, and thus the prime management factor, held sway well into the twentieth century. The role of managers was to recruit suitable workers, and then calculate work patterns so that the rate for the job equated to the scientifically-calculated amount of work that should be achieved. Those who failed to meet their targets received less pay and would be eventually dismissed. Those who over-achieved would receive more pay and greater security of work. If all the workers over-achieved, then the targets were too low and would be raised. All workers received the same treatment. This scientific management program suited simple manufacturing tasks requiring more brawn than brains. As women were physically not as strong as men, they were paid less. Scientific management is still used in basic manufacturing today, especially in the fashion industry.

As the twentieth century progressed, jobs became more technologically complicated and the workforce became better educated as universal education for all became the norm throughout much of the industrialized word. Research by Elton Mayo at the Hawthorne plant of Western Electric in Chicago, between 1924 and 1932, began to cast doubts on the universal applicability of scientific management. Mayo found that work conditions, social factors, and group dynamics were also important factors in worker behavior.

The Hawthorne studies showed the complexity of motivation. Later research using US managers, by Frederick Herzberg, published in 1962, suggested that whilst insufficient money was a demotivator for management grades, it was factors such as achievement and recognition that most motivated those at this stage of their careers. Money, it is true, is a facilitator, and everyone requires enough for their basic needs, but the actual motivational factors operating on an individual may be as diverse as the work population. Herzberg concluded that there were factors which led to satisfaction, and thus motivated people – he termed these **Motivators** – and that there were other factors which did not motivate, but, if they were absent, led to dissatisfaction and thus to demotivation – he termed these **Hygiene Factors**. His results are summarized in Table 3.1.

Table 3.1

Motivators *presence of which leads to satisfaction*	Hygiene Factors *absence of which leads to dissatisfaction*
Achievement	Policy and administration
Recognition	Supervision
Work issues	Relationships
Responsibility	Work environment
Advancement	Salary
Growth	Personal life
	Status
	Security

Herzberg's findings are useful in another context within the management of diversity – the spending life-cycle of an individual.

Consider young people starting out on a new job. They may well live at home, or in cheap rented accommodation, and while they will be expected to contribute to household expenses, much of their disposable income will be spent on fashion items and personal assets. This phase of the spending cycle can be termed **EARN and SPEND**.

A few years later, they are in long-term relationships, and may be considering settling down and perhaps buying a home. At this stage their spending pattern changes to **EARN and SAVE**. It may well be that every spare cent goes straight into a savings account.

As their careers develop and their incomes increase, they will have more disposable income. If they have no children they may well have become DINKYs (Double income, no kids yet), and may revert to **EARN and SPEND**. If they do have children, there will be a need for them to revert to saving again for the costs of their children's college or university costs and maybe even weddings, or for their own retirement, but the pattern is likely to be **EARN – SAVE SOME – SPEND SOME**.

Once the children set up on their own, the parents can **SPEND and DE-SAVE**, i.e. use their savings to improve their quality of life. The so-called gray dollar, pound, etc., has become very important in the marketing programs of a large range of goods and services, and has developed its own sector of operations. Carnival Cruises in the US, the world's largest cruise company, best known for its fun-packed *Carnival* brand targeted at the younger age range, also operates Holland-America Cruises, an operation best known for catering for the retired vacationer. In the UK, the Saga Group markets vacation, insurance and other products solely to those over 50 (although they can take a partner aged over 40 with them).

The modern approach to management is a contingency approach, in which the methods and tools of management are not fixed, but are contingent upon the situation. What works well in one company may fail in another. What is applicable to one group of workers may cause resentments in a different group. In the spending life-cycle described above, extra money earned through overtime may well motivate a person saving for a first home, but be less attractive to older workers who wish to spend quality leisure time with their families. For them, recognition may be much more of a motivator.

As work forces have become more diverse, managers need to recognize that employees inhabit a series of worlds: there is the world of work, there is the country of which they are citizens, and there is their cultural world. These worlds may have very different values, and these values may be in conflict. Good employers and managers should be aware of this and take account of such values wherever possible in the workplace. As organizations become more and more global (*see* Chapter 5), the onus is on the organization and its managers to ensure that when it is operating in another culture, it does so in a manner that is in tune with that culture.

The earliest methods of dealing with a diverse workforce contained a degree of 'ghettoization'.

Ghettos have been used since ancient times to confine those minority groups that a society finds useful in terms of skills, but whose culture it did not want to absorb. Even today, there are areas within cities that are populated by particular groups. New York was long known for its different areas, each with its own culture and where the daily language might be Yiddish, Italian, Armenian or Mandarin/Cantonese. Ghettos always carry the risk that their inhabitants are less likely to mix with the indigenous population, which therefore does not get to know and understand them. This makes them ready scapegoats for unscrupulous politicians. Far better and more effective is a society that allows everybody to live side by side, all retaining their own customs. Organizations need to ensure that they do not create actual or virtual ghettos by placing minorities together. The danger of stereotyping, conscious or unconscious, is all too real, and can create virtual ghettos if all the members of a particular group are funneled into similar jobs.

Modern management theory considers that what a person *is* should not be important; it is what they can *do* and can *contribute* to the organization that matters. The work of Meredith Belbin mentioned earlier, and to be covered in Chapter 6, is important in the context of requiring managers to concentrate on the synergy to be gained from diversity, rather than the problems that can occur when everybody thinks and acts the same way.

The successful manager values the contribution that diversity can bring, even if it makes the management task a little harder. A diverse workforce means that much more attention needs to be given to the individual and to his or her needs and wants. The pay-off is a workforce in which people feel valued for who they are, and in which people are motivated and thus more productive. In just about a century, management has gone from Taylor's ideas of everybody being treated the same, to the current situation in which diversity is welcomed, and people are treated equitably whatever their background or status. Equity is not the same as equality. Whilst the Concise Oxford Dictionary defines *equal* as 'the same', the definition of the word *equity* begins with fairness. If people are to give their best, they need to believe that they are respected as individuals and that they are being treated fairly. An oft-quoted phrase, which probably had its origins in the military, is "you don't have to like your boss, but you do need to trust him or her." Trust grows out of fairness.

The ease of travel in the modern world, and the development of formal economic/political groupings such as the EU (European Union)

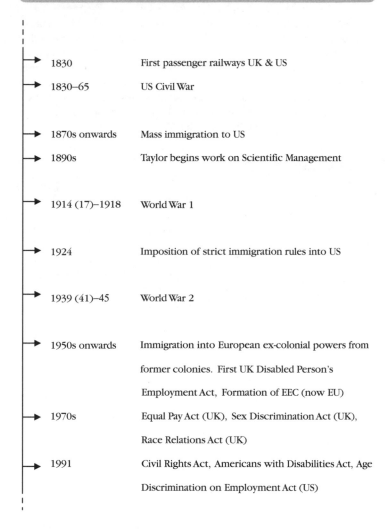

1830	First passenger railways UK & US
1830–65	US Civil War
1870s onwards	Mass immigration to US
1890s	Taylor begins work on Scientific Management
1914 (17)–1918	World War 1
1924	Imposition of strict immigration rules into US
1939 (41)–45	World War 2
1950s onwards	Immigration into European ex-colonial powers from former colonies. First UK Disabled Person's Employment Act, Formation of EEC (now EU)
1970s	Equal Pay Act (UK), Sex Discrimination Act (UK), Race Relations Act (UK)
1991	Civil Rights Act, Americans with Disabilities Act, Age Discrimination on Employment Act (US)

Fig. 3.1 Time-line.

and NAFTA (North American Free Trade Association), with the rights of movement of labor between member states, have all further diversified the workforces of many organizations. Indeed the EU has already begun to legislate for equality of treatment throughout its member states, through such measures as the European Union Working Time Directive and the European Social Charter. Reference material for EU employment policies can be found in Richard Pettinger's book *The European Social Charter* (*see* Chapter 9).

KEY LEARNING POINTS

» The nature of society has changed to provide more choice to employees by freeing them from the need to live in close proximity to their workplace.

» People are motivated by a variety of factors, of which money is just one.

» Motivational factors may alter for each individual during a career.

» Equity and equality are not the same. The former is about fairness; the latter concerned with sameness.

The E-Dimension in Managing Diversity

» Mutual understanding lies at the heart of managing diversity. Improved ICT, using the synergy of the telephone, e-mail, and the Internet, can make it much easier for organizational communications to reach the most remote parts of the organization speedily and efficiently.
» Managers need to be aware, however, of the dangers of isolation and a lack of a personal approach, and must recognize that these can be demotivators to members of staff.
» No matter where a member of staff is located, ICT should be used sensitively to weld the organization together, and every opportunity should be taken to show employees that they are recognized and valued.

At the heart of managing diversity is mutual understanding. The more people from diverse backgrounds, even with widely differing experiences, work together, the more they are likely to realize that their similarities are far greater than any differences. Shakespeare put this into words in *The Merchant of Venice* when the Jew Shylock exclaims, "If you prick me, do I not bleed?" – i.e. I am as human as you are. One of the many disturbing aspects of genocide is the manner in which the perpetrators attempt to justify their actions by trying to dehumanize their victims to make them appear radically different.

As organizations become more and more global in their operations, staff need to be managed across an increasing large geographic area. Globalization and the management of diversity form the subject of Chapter 5: this chapter concentrates on the use of the Internet and on electronic communications in the management of diversity.

The Internet began with the linking together of a series of computers in the US Defense Agency Research Projects Administration (DARPA) to form what became known in 1969 as ARPAnet, and was designed to protect military communications in the event of a nuclear attack – a very real fear in the international political climate of the time. The system used three university hosts in California and one in Utah. Later, in the 1970s, the US academic community set up a purely civilian network funded by the National Science Foundation (NSF) which linked an increasing number of US and foreign universities via NSFnet. For the first time academics and researchers throughout the world could communicate text via a new medium – electronic mail, rapidly contracted to e-mail.

Students who had used e-mail at university then began to take up positions within the private sector, and it was not long before large commercial organizations in the US, beginning with computer companies such as IBM and Hewlett-Packard, began to talk to each other via e-mail, linking their systems to the NSFnet.

In 1993, Marc Andreesen and his group at the University of Illinois introduced the first web browser software (called Mosaic), which was a software application for the UNIX operating system, but was later adapted for Apple Macintosh and for Microsoft Windows®. NSFnet gradually became less relevant and the commercial world saw the birth of Internet Service Providers (ISPs): by the middle of the 1990s, organizations in both the public and private sectors were not only using e-mail, but were beginning to design and post web pages. The World Wide Web (WWW) had been born.

In terms of the management of diversity, the main implications of the Internet have been in communications. Other titles in the ExpressExec series deal with the more commercial aspects of the Internet within business, but internally the Internet and e-mail have revolutionized both internal communications and the critical supplier/organization interface.

The power of Information and Communications Technology (ICT) is less in the attributes of the individual components, computers, telephones, radio transmission, cameras, etc., than in the synergy that can be obtained when these components are used in conjunction with each other.

One of the difficulties of managing a diverse workforce is that unless the individuals all share one physical space, part of the communications process is nearly always lost – that of body language. As highly visual animals, humans acquire up to 80% of their information about the world through vision. It is actually extremely difficult for people to disguise how they are feeling from those who can see them; indeed, those in the acting profession need special training in order to be able convince audiences that their emotions are 'real'. If an employee is unhappy, a glance at his or her face and posture may say exactly that, despite whatever words he or she may utter. Similarly, if someone expresses verbal agreement but is subtly shaking his or her head at the same time, a sensitive manager will believe the body language clue rather than the verbal statement, and realize that the person does not agree at all.

E-mail, for all its usefulness, tends to be a very curt method of communication. There are protocols for expressing emotion, but the accepted symbol for a smile conveys nothing like the impact of an actual smile.

The use of video-conferencing as a device to link sites which are huge distances apart has grown rapidly in recent years, aided by the availability of PC-top cameras which use Windows® software and operate through the Internet. Even with the best picture definition available, however, the body language clues can be difficult to pick up. The pixel definition even of the most expensive technology is never as good as the human eye. There also tends always to be a very tiny time lag between exchanges on a video-conferencing system, and this delay further confuses the interpretation of the visual clues.

Where the Internet has proved to be a great boon is in the area of corporate dissemination and in its ability to contribute to the formation of diverse multi-functional teams. The linking of suppliers into the design system computers at Boeing (*see* Chapter 7) greatly enhanced the sense of teamwork and ownership both for workers from Boeing and for its subcontractors who were building the Boeing 777 in the early 1990s. Team members were able to move drawings around and bounce ideas off colleagues with an ease that would have been considered science fiction just a few years earlier. Many of those team members were from different backgrounds and cultures, employed in organizations across the globe, but they were able to act in harmony due to the incredibly efficient communications links between them.

Colin Hastings and his colleagues in the UK have stressed the importance of managing 'the team apart' in their work on superteams. ICT can help to ensure that all members of a team or project group are as fully informed as possible about all developments.

Members of staff may have such diversity that they are working in a different language. More and more organizational web sites are being produced in the main languages of those who use them. An organization such as the EU (European Union) employs staff from all member countries speaking many different languages. The EU information site at www.europa.eu.int is accessible in Danish, Dutch, English, Finnish, French, German, Greek, Italian, Portuguese, Spanish, and Swedish, allowing the vast majority of EU staff (and citizens) to access the Union's web pages and keep themselves up to date.

HOME WORKING

ICT has added to the diversity of the workforce by allowing groups who previously had difficulty in being able to work at conventional jobs access to the employment market. Those who have to care for young children, sick or elderly relatives, or the disabled, and those living in remote areas, can find opportunities, especially for part-time work, by adding a PC, a modem, a fax machine and perhaps a PC-top camera to their home office. There are many tasks, especially within the service sector, that do not require regular attendance at an actual office in the conventional sense.

The isolation that home working can cause has become apparent in the past few years. It is not a method of working that suits everyone. The work of Elton Mayo described in Chapter 3 brought into focus the social aspects of work, and these can be completely denied to those working from home if they have little or no face-to-face contact with colleagues and must rely mainly on e-mail for their communications. In some parts of northern Scotland the concept of a tele-cottage has been pioneered. In a tele-cottage, a group of those who would normally work at home for different organizations meet to carry out their tasks in a convenient local central point. The tele-cottage can be fitted out with the latest in ICT, and there can be benefits in the purchase of equipment from sharing, as well as economies of scale. Such developments also often attract government funding, since they serve to improve the local economy by providing much-needed jobs.

The importance of ensuring that such remote members of staff feel part of the organization cannot be stressed too strongly. The danger of isolation acting as a demotivator is very real. Even a telephone call to give a remote and isolated employee a chance to hear an 'organizational message' can be very beneficial, and far more effective than relying on e-mails and messages on the organizational web site.

WELDING THE ORGANIZATION TOGETHER

One of the first features of globalization was the setting up of sites in other regions and countries. As these were largely self-contained, the workforce within them was likely to be fairly homogenous.

The use of ICT now allows organizations to disperse discrete functions. India has found itself a ready market for trained data-processing staff. Due to time differences, it is possible for an organization in the US or Europe to download data to India and have it processed there, where the quality is high and local wage rates tend to be lower. Much airline ticketing is carried out this way.

Organizations such as British Airways (BA) operate a major ticketing operation in the UK, but also at the Bulova Center in Queens, New York, where BA is one of the largest employers, if not the largest. New York is five hours behind London, so when it is evening in London, BA is able to reduce ticketing staff in the UK and transfer calls to New York, where it is still early afternoon. Of course, London-based staff start work five hours before New York, and so the system can be reversed and London can take New York's early morning bookings. As the booking computers are linked, the customer will remain unaware of the difference, in these days of local and toll-free telephone calls. Such an operation does make it important that the staff at such locations understand the cultural and language nuances of the customers, so as to present an effective and seamless web of service. It is interesting to consider the question of where do you work when your telephone is in New York, but you are booking a customer on a flight from London to Glasgow.

Any organization using ICT in this way needs to ensure that no matter where members of staff work, and no matter what their job, language, and culture, they are still made to feel that they are an integral part of the organization. Herzberg's work on motivation covered in Chapter 3 stressed the importance of recognition. Managers need to ensure that staff realize that they are recognized and appreciated. The anthropologist, former curator of London Zoo, and author of *The Naked Ape* (1967) and *Manwatching* (1978), Desmond Morris once produced a list of Ten Golden Rules for leaders of primate groups and, as was stated in Chapter 2, human beings are primates. One of those rules was that the leaders of groups should go around and reassure their extreme subordinates from time to time. A number of senior managers (perhaps the more sensitive ones) have realized that this cannot always be accomplished by using the Internet or e-mail, and that an annual visit around the organization, or attendance at social or sports functions, can be very cost effective when the impact on motivation is taken into consideration. Even if this is not possible, a hand-written note, particularly one saying 'thank you' or 'well done', implies a personal touch that an e-mail message simply cannot convey. Such notes are often treasured and shown to family and friends, and can have a considerable motivational influence.

BEST PRACTICE

Given the importance of face-to-face contact, including an ability to use body language to gain clues about real thinking, it is not surprising that the use of the Internet is at an early stage when it comes to managing staff. It is doubtful whether any court or tribunal would look kindly upon the hiring and especially firing of staff purely by e-mail at the moment.

There are organizations, however, where the staff are so widely scattered that the sheer geography of the situation makes the use of electronic communications not just a useful tool, but a key part of the organization's ability to function and survive.

One such organization is the University of the Highlands and Islands (UHI) in Scotland. Set up in the 1990s as a project linking the further education colleges in the north of Scotland (plus a number of specialist institutions) the UHI now has over 20 sites stretching from the Shetland islands in the north, through the city of Inverness at the northern end of Loch Ness, to the ancient capital of Scotland, Perth, further south and to the island of Lewis in the Outer Hebrides to the West. With hundreds of staff in support, technical and academic roles, the UHI has only a small central staff at its executive office; most staff being out in the colleges. These institutions retain their independence and their local identity whilst being part of a federal university. Students can study close to home without having to travel many miles across mountainous and difficult country. Travel in the north of Scotland can be very expensive with a flight from Aberdeen to Shetland costing nearly as much as one from London to New York; in such circumstances technology is being used to obviate the need for staff to travel.

The UHI has its own dedicated telephone system that is used for both telephone and visual communications. Much use is made of video-conferencing using a multi-link system that allows multiple sites to video-conference with one another. The whole system uses an Integrated Services Digital Network (ISDN 6) telephone network, ensuring the highest possible quality of visual reproduction. In addition to the main video-conference suites on the component sites, increasing numbers of staff have video cameras attached to their personal computers enabling them to video-conference from their own desks using Windows® software.

An important objective for the UHI is to ensure that all staff feel a sense of ownership and of belonging. The video-conferencing and e-mail systems (using GroupWise) are used for staff communication, teaching and tutorials. Despite the body language problems mentioned earlier in this chapter, the technology has proved a boon in bringing staff together without the need to travel. There are no motorways/freeways north of Perth and many of the main roads are single carriageway. The railways are also single track between the main stations. Thus travel times can be very long and time-consuming. For staff to be able to meet electronically has been important in bringing a diverse workforce together to meet common goals and objectives. The benefits to students of being able to access tutors across the network cannot be understated.

Further communication is achieved using the UHI web site, where UHI information, course details and press releases are available.

The UHI has support from both the central UK government in London and the Scottish Executive and parliament in Edinburgh, with extra financial support coming from local authorities, the National Lottery and the European Union. In 2001 the UHI gained Higher Education Institute status and is now actively working towards full university status. It offers an increasing number of courses, most of which can be studied locally, thus enhancing the local economy.

Whilst the UHI is still at an early stage in its development, there is no doubt that the creative use of ICT to bring together a diverse group to act as one, but still to retain loyalty to their home institutions, has been a major factor in its success up to now.

The UHI web site can be found at: www.uhi.ac.uk

KEY LEARNING POINTS

» The more people know about each other, the more they will understand each other.

» The Internet and ICT in general have aided the globalization process by improving communications.
» Isolation and a lack of recognition can be demotivators; the personal touch is still very important.
» ICT now allows not just whole operations, but individual functions to be located at the most advantageous site.

The Global Dimension of Managing Diversity

» Globalization has grown as communications and transportation links have increased.
» As organizations become more global, so they and their indigenous staff need to take on board the cultures and the social customs of the areas in which they wish to operate.
» The cultural issues may include hierarchies, gender, the family, age, social structure, disability, the relative influence of the state versus the individual, religion, and legal issues affecting employment. These issues are also referred to in Chapter 6.
» Language is a vital feature of business, and it is important to understand that there are many variations of widely-used languages.

The ease of both physical and electronic communication and transportation has greatly aided the process of globalization. Globalization is not new. The Morgan Combine set up by J P Morgan in the US in the late nineteenth and early twentieth centuries operated in a number of countries, often hiding its true ownership behind local organizations. In a development that may have surprised many, the Internet has not only aided large organizations in the penetration of global markets, but has also rejuvenated many small organizations, especially in the retail sector, which can now market and sell globally at a fraction of the cost they would have incurred prior to the development of the World Wide Web. Whilst there are now many organizations that operate within a global market, there are fewer that can actually be described as truly global organizations. To be truly global, an organization needs not only to be selling in an international market, but also to have a firm base of operations within that market. In effect, the inhabitants of the market possibly believe that the organization is actually a home grown one. Examples of such truly global organizations include Ford, General Motors, Coca-Cola, Shell (whose complete name is Royal Dutch Shell), and Cable Network News (CNN).

One of the major problems of globalization is highlighted by Philip Harris and Robert Moran in *Managing Cultural Differences* (1979) and relates to a perceived lack of empathy. It is not unusual for senior managers of organizations that are expanding globally to find that they are now managing staff from acquired companies that have developed in a completely different culture. Unless both sides have given careful study and consideration to the ways in which the other works and thinks, i.e. the different cultural contexts, there is always the danger that misunderstandings will affect the building of a positive relationship. As mentioned in earlier chapters, an understanding of the cultural background should form part of the planning for all those who are involved in the globalization process. As listed in Chapter 9, writers such as Harris and Morris in the US, Richard Lewis in the UK, and Fons Trompenaars in the Netherlands have produced extremely useful information and guides on the manner of doing business in other countries and working with those from other cultures. Companies that operate globally, such as British Airways, provide cultural orientation training for staff before they are sent on a foreign posting. A considerable part of that training is devoted to the avoidance of unintentionally giving offense.

In many cases, it may be that those cultures that appear nearest in values, attitudes and beliefs to the organization's home culture are the most problematic in this respect, as there may be a temptation to assume that people's behavior will be similar to that with which the organization is familiar. In the early days of television advertising, a number of US companies attempted to use their US advertisements on UK television, only to find that whilst the language may be very similar, the culture of the advertising message was very different. Today, such advertisements are tailored to the particular culture in which they are to be shown, at least in the words used if not also in the images.

A highly popular series of Nescafé Gold Blend coffee advertisements was first screened in the UK. The format was based on a US TV series called *Moonlighting*, in which one of the sub-plots involved a 'will they, won't they?' romantic situation. The advertisements featured the build up to a romance, beginning with a young couple meeting by chance. So popular did these advertisements become that the next 'instalment' of the story would itself be advertised, with the screening time, in newspapers for a day or two before it was first shown. It may have been one of the few cases of viewers watching a television show with the intention of seeing an advertisement, rather than the other way round. However, when the advertisement was transferred to the US market, it was necessary to change the actors and the situation to one more in tune with US audiences' expectations and attitudes.

At number 17 in the Channel 4/Sunday Times list of Greatest TV Ads, published in the UK in 2000, was a Carling Black Label (a lager/lite beer) 'Dambusters' advertisement, a spoof based on the movie *The Dam Busters* (1954) which commemorated a famous World War II bombing raid carried out in 1943 on German dams in the industrial Ruhr valley by the RAF's 617 Squadron, using the famous 'bouncing bomb' technique designed by Barnes Wallis. That wartime incident has become part of British folklore, and the implications of the advertisement were well understood by the target audience – although how it would have been received in Germany or Austria is open to question. Even in the US, despite the wartime ally relationship, and the success of the British movie, it would probably be quite baffling to most viewers.

CULTURAL ISSUES

The actual specifics of different cultures that need to be taken into account in the management of diversity form the main content of the Chapter 6, which considers the current state of the management of diversity.

Managers operating in a global environment need to recognize that different parts of the world may well have different attitudes and value systems in respect of

» hierarchies
» gender
» the family
» age
» social structure
» disability
» the relative influence of the state v the individual
» religion
» legal issues affecting employment.

It may be very difficult for a manager from the US or Europe to appreciate the different social structures operating in a very diverse country such as India, where the caste system still exists and may have implications for organizational hierarchies. In many parts of India, organizations operate on a purely western model, but it is still possible to find more remote areas where other social systems are prevalent.

In many areas, family business ties are much stronger than those in the west and this needs to be taken into account when addressing staffing issues. The issue of gender and the status of women can be very problematic for managers in certain areas. There are still parts of the world where women are banned from education and work, and even from driving. Whilst the number of such areas is declining, they still exist and may present a cultural dilemma for a manager from the west, or for a western organization imbued with concepts of gender equality.

In the US, and to an extent in other western countries, the government tends to maintain a hands-off role in relation to business, although it is difficult to find any government that is totally uninvolved in commerce. The trend throughout the later years of the twentieth century was for many governments to privatize state enterprises. There are, however, still places where there is a considerable reliance on nationalized commercial activities, and as these are often run on highly bureaucratic principles it is necessary for managers to understand how a bureaucratic structure operates.

The most effective method of ensuring successful globalization is for an organization to study the cultures in which it wishes to operate, and then to consider the underlying reasons why certain things are done in particular ways. There are often good reasons associated with nature, or with social organization, why a culture operates as it does. Cows are considered special in India because of their importance as a source of milk, vital in a country with an arid climate in many of its regions. A cow is a much-prized and valuable possession because, in the past, its well-being could well have meant the difference between life or death through starvation for a family – hence the respect still given to the animal. What might seem strange in Times Square makes perfect sense in Bombay!

Even the names of products may need to be changed. The Volkswagen Golf car has been known as the Rabbit in the US – a name apparently unacceptable to European drivers – whilst the Fiat Ritmo of the 1970s was renamed the Strada in the UK, as the name Ritmo conjured up an image of a lawnmower to UK consumers. Rolls Royce's Silver Mist model cannot be sold in German-speaking countries under that name, since *mist* has an offensive and vulgar meaning in German. Many manufactures now seek safety from the risk of causing offense by using an invented, irrelevant, generic (often meaningless) name such as Neon (Chrysler), or Mondeo (Ford), or even for numbers, such as the Boeing 747 or Airbus A330. Even so, one major US airline refused to buy the Boeing 707 because of the CEO's superstition about the numbers, and only purchased the product when a new version designated the 720 was introduced.

RELIGION

Whilst many countries are now largely secular, in others religion is still very influential. Indeed the later years of the twentieth century saw a rise of fundamentalist Muslim religious groups gaining political power with very determined religious, social and political agendas – something which is still growing. Even in the US, the politics of certain areas have been influenced by religious beliefs – as can be seen in the so-called Bible Belt.

Religious beliefs can be one of the most influential parts of a culture and managers need to understand their influence, and learn how to avoid giving offense.

LANGUAGE

The major commercial language in the world is English, but there are a number of versions of English, each with its own grammar, spelling and meaning of many words. Microsoft Word®, a word processing program used throughout the world, lists no fewer than 62 separate languages in the Word95® spell and grammar-check utility. Of these, there were multiple versions of Dutch, French, Italian and Portuguese, fifteen variants of Spanish, plus Catalan and Basque, and no fewer than nine variants of English, including British English, United States English, and even Canadian English.

The large number of television and movie offerings in various forms of English means today that, most of the time, native English speakers are able to cope with the variations. Even so, if you ask an American to describe a vest and suspenders you will receive a very different description from one given by somebody from the UK. In the UK a vest is an undergarment for the top half of the body, whilst a vest in the US is a waistcoat; suspenders are worn by British ladies to hold up their stockings, while braces hold up men's trousers, and are not usually deployed on children's teeth – although in its singular form the word can be used in that context! No wonder Sir Winston Churchill once described Britain and the US as "two countries divided by a common language".

When working with staff who normally use another language, or even variant of the manager's own language, it is always wise for a manager to seek feedback to ensure that the words used have identical meanings to each party.

LEGAL ISSUES

Legal issues can be a minefield in a global operation. Governments are, naturally, normally very particular that their laws apply on their territory. US managers operating in Europe need to be aware that European Union law is superior to the national law of member states. Equally, managers from other countries who are working in the US may be unused to a system where State law is so strong, allowing, for example, the death penalty in some States but not in others.

BEST PRACTICE

The world cruise industry catered for 9.4 million vacationers in 1999 (of whom 6.25 million were from the US, nearly 0.75 million from the UK and one million from Asia, including Japan) compared with 5.4 million in 1992; a growth rate that would be the envy of many industries.

Princess Cruises of Los Angeles form part of the P&O Group of companies from the UK but its operation is designed primarily for the US customers who make up the vast majority of the Princess customer base. Princess was acquired in 1974, when its US founder sold it to P&O which was attempting to gain a penetration of the growing US cruise vacation market. The company became well known through the *Love Boat*® television series that featured one of its vessels.

The crew of any cruise ship operating today is likely to be multi-cultural, and more and more the customers will be equally as diverse. It is important to the customers that the crew are culturally attuned to the needs and wants of the customer.

On one particular Princess ship, the *Royal Princess*, there were no fewer than twelve different nationalities of crew and twelve separate nationalities of customers on board. The crew included US, UK, West Indian, Filipino, Indian and Pakistani citizens, and whilst the majority of the customers were from the US, there were sizeable UK and Canadian contingents, plus Central and South Americans and other Western Europeans.

In the 1990s, Princess Cruises adopted a customer service credo entitled CRUISE, which stood for Courtesy, Respect, Unfailing In Service and Excellence.

The CRUISE program had a cornerstone statement of, "At one point in every day, one of our customers will come into contact with one of us, the Princess employees, and at that moment in time we will be Princess Cruises. Our entire reputation as a company will be in our hands and we will make an impression. The impression will either be good or it will be bad and we will have spoken to our customer more loudly than all our community involvement, all our advertising and all our public relations put together."

(*Source*: Princess Cruises CRUISE Program information to customers)

The ten points of the Princess Service Credo, included in the documentation provided for customers, were

1 **We strive to be the very best**. We do the best job we are capable of all the time in every part of the ship. We are proud of what we do.

2 **We react** quickly to resolve passenger problems immediately. We do everything possible to please our passengers.

3 **We smile; we are on stage**. We always maintain positive eye contact and use our service vocabulary. We greet our passengers: we tell them 'certainly,' and 'I will be happy to do so,' and 'it will be a pleasure'.

4 **We are friendly, helpful and courteous**. It is the Princess way. We treat our fellow passengers and crew members as we would like to be treated ourselves.

5 **We are ambassadors of our cruise ship** when at work and at play. We always speak positively and never make negative comments.

6 **Our uniforms are immaculate**. We wear proper and safe footwear that is clean and polished and we wear our nametags. We take pride and care in our personal grooming.

7 **We are positive**. We always find a way to get it done. We always try to make it happen. We never, never give up.

8 **We use proper telephone etiquette**. We always try to answer within three rings and with a smile in our voice. If necessary, we always ask if we may place callers on hold, and we eliminate call transfers whenever possible.

9 **We are knowledgeable** about all cruise ship information and always recommend the shipboard services.

10 **We never say 'no.'** We say 'I will be pleased to check and see'. We suggest alternatives. We call our supervisor or manager if we feel we cannot satisfy our passengers' needs.

(*Source*: Princess Cruises CRUISE Program information to customers)

Some of these points might have less priority in some cultures than in others, as anybody who has traveled widely will know. The point made to staff is that these were the culturally accepted norms of the customers and therefore must be the priority for staff.

In particular, the whole credo requires the crew to use English when they are on stage, even if talking amongst themselves. It is appreciated that this can be difficult, because at times of stress it is natural to slip into one's native tongue. Nevertheless, a customer may well feel uncomfortable or even intimidated to hear the staff speaking in a way that cannot be understood – after all they *may* be talking about the customer.

By adopting a credo which recognizes the need for staff to respect the customer's culture, Princess Cruises have been able to increase the customer base and gain a high reputation for excellent customer service.

KEY LEARNING POINTS

» Globalization is about culture not geography.
» The way something is done in a particular culture is likely to relate to the attitudes, values, beliefs, and history of the people of that culture.
» The meaning of words can differ significantly between different variants of what is apparently the same language.

The State of the Art of Managing Diversity

» Different cultures have different facets that may affect the way business is conducted.

» Contingency theory suggests that there is no single best method of managing – a manager should use the techniques best suited to the situation and the people involved.

» Organizations develop their own cultures, and these need to be recognized and understood.

» Cultural change is slow and generational.

» Migrations in the twentieth century led to much greater diversity within the workplace.

» The roles in the workplace of women, the disabled and the more elderly have changed, and equity has become the objective.

» Men and women are different, but complementary, in terms of employment.

» Team role theory suggests that a diverse group may be more effective than a homogenous one.

» It is possible to legislate against discrimination, but there is a need to educate against prejudice.

There are several types of diversity that must exercise the mind of a contemporary manager. Cultural diversity was considered in Chapter 5 and will be expanded upon in this chapter. In addition, social changes have increased the scale of diversity even within relatively homogenous work groups by the increasing employment of women, older people and the disabled. All of these groups are able to add synergy to the organization.

This chapter will consider first the current cultural situation, and then look at gender, age and disability.

CULTURE AND MANAGING DIVERSITY

When Taylor began to articulate his ideas of scientific management in the early twentieth century he was followed by other workers in the US, the UK and other parts of northern Europe. One thing they all had in common was the conviction that the Anglo-Saxon/Nordic (which included the US) ways of doing things were the best for the whole world. It is hardly surprising that they came to this conclusion, since they all had similar cultural roots.

The contingency concept of management is prevalent today (*see* Chapter 2). Contingency theory suggests that there is no single best method of managing – each manager should use the techniques best suited to each particular situation and to the people involved, and should recognize that there may be different methods of achieving objectives, depending on the organization, the people and the culture that he or she is working with.

Although the word *culture* is often used to mean different things, in organizational terms the simple definition based on the previous chapters is, 'The way things are done around here'. From this definition, which is also useful for defining national cultures, it can be discerned that there may well be different ways of doing the same thing. It is important to note that, in many cases, a particular way is not better than that chosen by another organization or even another national group – it is just different. Different does not imply a judgement; it is purely a statement of fact. In the US, manslaughter often carries a twenty-year prison sentence; in the UK this period may be much less. No one has the right to infer from this difference that the US is right and the UK wrong, or vice versa. They are just different, and have adopted different procedures and laws to suit their national cultures and attitudes. The US and the UK are often compared because, in many instances, the cultural roots are the same, and Britons and Americans think and act very similarly much of the time; there are, however, some major cultural differences between them.

Culture is something that develops over long periods of time and is transmitted from one generation to the next. In the context of national cultures, this is done within the family structure, from parents to children, and within schools, through the education system. Organizational culture is transmitted from longer-serving staff to new employees and through induction programs, corporate events, publications, and other techniques.

Modern methods of managing cultural diversity seek not so much to impose an alien regime, but to combine the best of the organization with the best of the host, whether the host is an actual country, or just those employees with a different background who have come into the organization.

ORGANIZATIONAL CULTURE

Organizational culture is a reflection of the way an organization operates and it often reflects the core values of the organization. Organizational cultures may be bureaucratic and role-related, as they are in many government and public sector organizations. They may be related more to power and to the influence of the most prominent individual within the organization, a situation often found in entrepreneurial organizations. There may be little formal structure, as in a partnership of lawyers of physicians, or there may be a matrix approach, in which knowledge and expertise are the most valued assets of the organization and bureaucracy is kept to a minimum.

It is not difficult to imagine the frustration that a rule-driven bureaucratic culture might experience when dealing with an entrepreneurial one where the influence and wishes of the owner or CEO take precedence over everything else. The former's rules may well be totally alien to the latter. It is perfectly possible for there to be different cultures operating within the same organization. An accounts department may resemble a bureaucratic culture, whilst research and development, with a more free-thinking head, may operate in a matrix mode. Never-theless, especially within the same organization, it is important that the cultures 'get on with each other', and this requires all the staff to have a knowledge of organizational culture.

Charles Handy, a regular contributor to work on organizational culture in both the US and the UK, has produced interesting models of organizational cultures, and his work is described in Chapter 8. In *The Gods of Management* (1978) he describes four types of organizational culture linked to the supposed attributes of four of the gods of ancient Greece, and he shows how an understanding of the possible tensions between organizational cultures can aid the management of diversity in the modern world.

It may well be that huge organizations actually have divisions or controlled subsidiaries that operate with different cultural norms, especially when they are situated in another country. Here again, understanding is the key to effective co-operation.

Every organization has to deal with those outside its own boundaries; indeed it is these relationships which form the foundation of this book. While an organization may be able to control the cultural behavior within itself to a degree, that of outside organizations may be completely beyond its control. Again, knowledge and a willingness to work together to overcome any cultural differences for mutual benefit are required. It is true throughout humanity that, however different we are, our similarities are normally much greater: this is also true of organizations. A willingness by all concerned to bend a little when necessary works wonders.

CULTURAL CHANGE

It was stated above there is a generational aspect to the transfer of culture. Cultural change too is often generational. It is easy for a senior management to announce that the culture of an organization is to change, but much less easy to achieve it in anything other than the long term. Values, attitudes and beliefs, whether personal, national or organizational, are deeply held – indeed wars are often fought over them and people may be willing to lay down their lives for them – so they can be changed only gradually, hence the concept of generational change. It is particularly important to realize that those who enter an organization from a different cultural background, whether it is from another national culture or just that they are coming from another organization, will be expected to undergo an overnight transformation into a new set of values. This process requires understanding, time and patience from managers. One very important step in the process is not only to tell people 'the way we do things around here,' but also to explain *why* things are done that way.

NATIONAL CULTURE

When Fons Trompenaars published *Riding the Waves of Culture* in 1993 and R.D. Lewis wrote *When Cultures Collide* in 2000, they provided valuable additions to the excellent work of Philip R. Harris and Robert T. Moran, from California and Arizona respectively, who produced the first edition *of Managing Cultural Differences* in 1979, with the fifth edition coming out in the twenty-first century.

As the world, especially the world of business, becomes smaller through the improved communications, so, paradoxically does the importance of understanding cultural diversity become more important. It has already been observed that cultural change is generational and responds at a much slower rate than technological change. Thus, whilst communications between different cultural groups are much quicker and much easier, the differences between those groups still remain. Only perhaps in the fields of popular culture such as pop music and international sport is there rapid global convergence on a single issue.

It stands to reason, therefore, that as organizations undertake their operations on an increasingly global basis and/or employ a more culturally diverse workforce, the need for cultural understanding becomes greater and greater.

Trompenaars set out to explore the cultural diversity aspects of business, and his work is recommended to the reader in the highest terms. He considered cultural diversity in terms of a series of differing attitudes held by various national groups. It should be noted that such attitudes are always just a general tendency – not all Americans will react in one way to a particular set of circumstances and not all Germans another – but his research did reveal a consistent series of national tendencies. The attitudes he believed were most critical were

» attitudes to time
» universal vs. particular
» individualism vs. collectivism
» emotional vs. neutral
» specific vs. diffuse
» achievement vs. ascription
» attitudes to the environment.

To these should be added attitudes to gender, age and disability.

None of these concepts is absolute: national tendencies lie on a continuum between the two extremes. In the following section, the various factors are described and, where appropriate, the cultures lying at each end and in the middle are given. Trompenaars spent many hours researching this, often by asking multiple choice questions requiring a response to a certain set of circumstances. For example, how much right does a friend have to expect you to lie for him or her in a certain set of circumstances. The replies he received to this particular question were interesting, since it was clear that in some cultures it is expected that friends will support one another come what may (a particular response), whilst in others, if a friend breaks the rules then those rules should apply whatever the circumstances (a universal response).

Attitude to time

It might be thought that time is a universal constant, as an hour is an hour is an hour whether in Los Angeles or Shanghai or Oxford. In looking at the cultural effect of time, however, it is not the absolute nature of time that is important, but the different attitudes towards it.

Eastern cultures often have a reverence for ancestors and historical precedent. The United States, according to the research, was less interested in the past and much more concerned about the future. In many Western cultures, punctuality is prized and the lack of it is considered bad manners, thoughtless and insulting. In other cultures, punctuality is given far less importance. This difference of attitude can immediately lead to a cultural clash in the workplace. If somebody comes to work in a culture where punctuality is important, say the

US, then they must respect that and be on time. It may be necessary to help them to develop that respect by pointing out how lateness can impact on schedules, upset work patterns and cause colleagues to waste time. Explanation often goes a long way to achieving the desired result. A US manager working in a culture where punctuality is less critical may well have to learn not to be stressed by it, but to adjust working practices to allow for it. Frustration on both sides is inevitable until the compromise is reached. Shouting is never the solution: you can shout as much as you like, but little will change!

Universal vs. particular

In some cultures, a set of rules or laws is universally applied (or so perceived wisdom tells us, despite the fact that there is sometimes one law for certain members of society and another for others). In other cultures, rules and norms may be applied depending on the circumstances. Trompenaars and other writers on culture have pointed out that relationships such as friendship may confer special rights and obligations in a particular culture, but are less welcome in a universal one. In a universal culture, an individual has much less right to expect a friend to cover up for him or her than in a culture where particularism is the accepted norm.

In general, the US and Japan display high levels of universalism when tested, whereas the former constituents of Yugoslavia and certain Far Eastern countries (excluding Japan) tended towards the particularism, although even in these countries it must be stressed that the overall tendency was that there should be universal rules applicable to everybody. This is perhaps a change that is having a global impact. Certain countries, such as the US and the UK, have strict rules against bribery, and anyone attempting to offer or accept bribes can expect to receive heavy punishment when caught. In many parts of the world such behavior is the norm, and those who do not indulge in it do not receive good service or treatment. They can also become objects of derision because of their unawareness of local practice.

In dealing with a culture at the particularism end of the spectrum, organizations need to know exactly which rules are being applied, by whom, and to whom.

Individualism vs. collectivism

Basically, people regard themselves either as members of a group first and as individuals second, or vice versa. Not surprisingly, the US is an individualism-oriented culture, whereas the Japanese came out, together with countries such as Nepal, East Germany under the communist regime, and other Far Eastern groupings, as tending towards a more collectivist approach. This should not be surprising given the political and social creeds of many eastern areas and of communism.

For those conducting business in other cultures, it is important to realize that it may be a group rather than a key individual which needs to be satisfied in a collectivist-oriented culture, and that the building of collective relationships will be of great importance.

Emotional vs. neutral

To what degree is it culturally acceptable to show personal feelings, especially in business relationships? In the US, UK, and Japan such revelations may be frowned on, less so in Italy and France. Latin cultures tend to accept displays of emotion more readily than those designated as Anglo-Saxon. Emotion is a good psychological safety valve; maybe this is part of the explanation for the apparently lower incidence of heart disease and other stress-related illnesses in Latin areas.

Whereas a display of emotion, and even temper, may be acceptable as a means of showing true feelings in Latin cultures, it is far less likely to produce effective results in North America, Northern Europe and the Far East, where the whole issue of 'face' can be very important. The British 'stiff upper lip' and Japanese inscrutability are examples of such concealed emotion.

Specific vs. diffuse

In many cultures, it is accepted, and expected, that there will be a personal relationship between those involved in business transactions, whereas in others the relationship is more between organizations than individuals, who are mere representatives of the organization. Position within the hierarchy may also be important in this respect in cultures where the hierarchy is itself important.

In some cultures, work and home are closely related; in others employees are not expected to bring domestic issues into their work place. This begs the question of how an individual is supposed to leave a problem at home – it is the *belief* that the two should not mix, and not the actual reality of the situation, that is important here. Trompenaars quotes China as a very diffuse culture, using the example of asking how many respondents would refuse to help their manager paint his home. In China, 72% would help whereas in the much more specific culture of the UK, only 8% would agree to give up their own time this way (the US figure was 11%). Similarly, in China 89% of employees believed that the organization had a responsibility to help to house its employees, compared to 55% of Japanese, but only 18% in the UK and 15% in the US. There has been a change of attitude on this issue in the US and the UK, since during the late nineteenth and early twentieth centuries, many organizations provided housing for staff.

An organization in a specific culture may appear, to those also adopting that culture as in-comers, to be much more focused on its objectives, whereas in a diffuse culture time may be spent talking about non-organizational related issues. Neither is right or wrong; both attitudes suit their cultures. It is again a matter of knowing, understanding and reacting in a culturally acceptable manner.

Achievement vs. ascription

An achievement-oriented culture confers status according to what people have done, whereas ascription is about position, connections and even birth. The US is the best example of an achievement-oriented culture, where it is believed that, with hard work and education, anybody can rise to the top. The careers of many early immigrants and their immediate descendants showed just what was possible. Achievement societies are more interested in *what* somebody studied, whereas ascription societies may be more concerned with *where* the studies occurred. In that respect, even the US, with its Ivy League of universities (Harvard, Yale and others), is not completely an achievement culture.

Titles and qualifications are much more important in ascription-oriented cultures, and great offense can be caused by omitting them or even by listing them incorrectly.

Attitudes to the environment

The extent that members of a culture believe that it is right and proper for mankind to try to control nature may well influence behavior and strategy at work. The developments in genetic engineering in the US and Europe suggest that these cultures believe that this research is acceptable. Trompenaars claimed that 35% in the UK and 38% in the USA believed that it is worth trying to control nature, compared with only 10% in Japan.

Environmental issues are now taken very seriously, and people are beginning to realize that interfering with nature can have potentially disastrous consequences, as global warming has shown. Countries which ignore internationally-agreed limits on chemical emissions are increasingly finding themselves under internal and external pressure to comply, as the US is now discovering.

There is also a related issue in the extent to which people feel they are the masters or mistresses of their own destinies. In the developed world, people do believe this far more than those living under communist regimes did. Controlling one's own destiny and controlling nature are closely linked, as is the concept of individualism versus collectivism. Fate, so important in many Eastern cultures, plays a much smaller role in the cultural psychology of the West.

MIGRATION

The migration of people from Europe to North America in the second half of the nineteenth and the early decades of the twentieth centuries was discussed in Chapter 3. Since the end of World War II, there has been considerable migration in order to seek a better economic life from the less-developed parts of the world into North America and Europe, and also from former communist regimes in Eastern Europe to the West. To these so-called economic refugees must be added those who have fled their own country as a consequence of war, famine and persecution. In the 1960s and 1970s, both Kenya and Uganda expelled large numbers of their citizens of Asian origin, many of whom were relocated, with UK government assistance, in the UK. Many of these East African Asians met an initially hostile reception from some parts of UK society, which were fearful of the social and economic impact of such an influx. In fact, the East African Asians brought excellent commercial skills with them, and Kenya's and Uganda's losses were the UK's gain, as many of them prospered and set up their own businesses. They brought a positive addition to the commercial and cultural diversity of the UK. At the same time, the Kenyan and Ugandan economies suffered as a result of the removal of some of their more entrepreneurial elements.

In the developed world, most governments have legislation in place to protect those entering society from outside from discrimination, a topic covered later in this chapter.

It is important for organizations to recognize that diversity may simply mean doing things differently. Different cultural groups may need special facilities for religious observance (although most of the world's major religions are pragmatic when it comes to balancing religious observance and work) and there may be the need for different food to be available – some cultures demand that food is slaughtered and prepared in a particular manner, halal and kosher for example. Body language and customs differ between groups, and mutual knowledge can save misunderstanding, embarrassment and offense.

If an organization is dealing with an ethnically diverse workforce, or is operating abroad, it must remember that just because people have migrated does not mean that they have lost their interest in their homeland. Political events and natural tragedies in the homeland may cause distress thousands of miles away; an empathetic approach from an employer will go a long way towards building respect. People may also bring their prejudices with them, and this needs to be taken into account when setting up teams and workgroups, although every attempt must be made to defuse potentially damaging attitudes.

WOMEN IN THE WORKPLACE

It is widely believed that it was the loss of a large proportion of the male population into the armies of the World War I that brought women into the workplace. This is a misconception; the war may have increased the number of women in employment and increased their skill base, but women had formed an important part of employment statistics long before 1914. Whilst the women in the upper echelons of medieval society may have lived lives of luxury and idleness, the lot of ordinary women was very different, and they formed an important and integral part of the economy, although in general they carried out different tasks from their menfolk.

Long established industries, such as coal mining and the cotton industry, had made considerable use of women and children, although public outcry led to the passing of a number of legislative measures to restrict this. For example, in the UK throughout the nineteenth century laws were passed banning the use of women and children in coal mines, outlawing the use of children as chimney sweeps, and eventually raising the age at which children could begin work. Whilst child labor is virtually unknown in the west, it has by no means been eradicated in less developed areas (as some global manufacturers have discovered), and it is an issue which attracts increasing concern from United Nations' agencies and international children's charities.

In a number of cultures, the role of women is restricted to domestic duties and the caring professions. In extreme cases, such as the Taliban regime in contemporary Afghanistan, women are forbidden to take any form of employment. The Taliban and their supporters claim that this is for religious reasons connected with modesty, although it may well have a great deal to do with the males in that culture protecting their power base. There are no logical reasons for the reluctance of many organizations to promote women to senior positions. The concept of a 'glass ceiling', inhibiting the progress of women, has been postulated by a number of writers, particularly Davidson and Cooper in *Shattering the Glass Ceiling* (1992) and Morrison and others in *Breaking the Glass Ceiling* (1994) (*see* Chapter 9). The progress towards sexual equality was painfully slow at times during the twentieth century; women in the UK did not gain full suffrage until the late 1920s, and equality of pay for similar work tasks did not become a statutory requirement until the Equal Pay Act of 1970.

One of the major developments in managing diversity has been the number of additional women entering employment through part-time jobs and the growth of the concept of job sharing. Originally developed in connection with lower-paid work, even some of the most high-powered jobs can be undertaken in this manner and this provides an antidote to often-quoted but erroneous ideas that child-care may inhibit effective performance by female workers. In the UK, numbers of women in the work place rose steadily in the twentieth century from 30% of the total workforce in 1911 to 42% in 1981, and the number of part-time workers from 47,000 males and 784,000 females in 1911 to 361,625 males and over 3 million females in 1981. The growth in part-time work, taking into account the huge rise in the UK population, has been dramatic and provides employers with access to a much wider and diverse skills base.

In the developed world, little gender differentiation exists in education and training, and it is in those areas that equality begins to have a marked and unalterable effect.

Based on work by Nigel Nicholson (*see* Chapter 9), it is possible to list some of the differences between men and women which must be taken into account in their employment. The use of the word 'tend' in this list is significant; there are no absolutes, and these differences are tendencies towards a particular end of a continuum.

» Men tend to be larger and stronger than a woman from the same culture
» Men tend to die earlier
» Men tend to lose their mental faculties at an earlier stage
» Men tend to be more promiscuous
» Men tend to be more competitive
» Men tend to be more self-interested
» Men tend to be more likely to take risks
» Men tend to play more games
» Men tend to be more interested in tools and weapons
» Men tend to be more single-minded
» Men tend to have better mental mapping skills.

On the other hand:

» Women tend to feel and express emotion more easily
» Women tend to be more emphatic
» Women tend to be more dexterous and less clumsy
» Women are more nurturing

» Women tend to have better social skills
» Women tend to have better verbal skills
» Women tend to be more co-operative
» Women are better at multi-tasking
» Women tend to have a better memory for object location
» Women tend to be better at spotting embedded objects.

The items in the second list have been connected with the biological role of women in childbearing. Females of the vast majority of species invest more of their time and resources in their young than do males. The advent of mass contraception has freed many women from having to consider sexual relations purely in terms of conception, and this has considerably altered social norms regarding sexual behavior.

Whilst the trend in the 1970s and 1980s was towards complete equality of men and women, thinking since then has been towards an equity that recognizes these differences and uses them constructively. John Gray's excellent book *Men are from Mars, Women are from Venus* celebrates the differences between the genders. It is important that men and women have equal treatment in pay and conditions at work, but women should be employed in roles that are best-suited both to the gender and to the individual. A female manager may do things differently, sometimes better than a man, sometimes worse perhaps, but, basically, as far as employment is concerned, if the job is done effectively, the manner in which it is done is of less importance.

Many of the old ideas that women could not do 'male' jobs have been proved fallacious, or removed by technology. There are now many female airline pilots and truck drivers. At one time both these jobs needed a degree of physical strength better provided by a man, but fly-by-wire and power steering/automatic transmissions have meant that strength is no longer a factor. The armed forces, particularly in Europe and North America, are still one area where there is considerable debate over the deployment of women in combat conditions. The Israeli armed forces, however, have used women as proactively and as effectively as men, especially when the country has been threatened by invasion.

The key to managing the diversity between male and female employees is to consider them not as opposites but as complementary to one another.

AGE AND DISABILITY

Two other types of diversity have become more common in the workplace through the increasing employment of those with disabilities and of those who have retired or been laid off from their original career.

Although employing a disabled worker may require some ergonomic adjustments, the motivation that the disabled often bring to their work can more than compensate for this. Many tasks can be performed just as competently by somebody who is disabled as by someone who is fully able and mobile. From a socially selfish point of view, every disabled person in employment is a relief to a government in terms of the need to supply care provision and financial allowances. It is always psychology better for people to be as self-sufficient as possible. It keeps their self-esteem high, and their work benefits as a result.

Older workers have been shown to be more reliable and more productive than younger employees. They generally have fewer potential distractions in their social lives and more highly developed attitudes to loyalty and team-working. Eastern culture places more reverence on age and experience than is found in the west. Many western executives laid off in their late 40s have come to feel that their working lives are at end and that younger successors are in greater demand than they are. There has, however, been a slow but growing trend for organizations to hire older workers in order to tap into their experience and motivation. Many of those taking early retirement now seek new careers, perhaps part-time, and they provide valuable extra diversity to their new employers, together with a deeper understanding of the world, and the way it works.

ROLE THEORY

Meredith Belbin in the UK has pioneered the concept of team roles. This concept states that teams should be composed of a series of diverse roles if they are to be effective. Team roles are described by Belbin as "... a pattern of behavior characteristic of the way in which one team member interacts with another where his performance serves to facilitate the progress of the team as a whole."

A full description of the roles and qualities Belbin has identified would take a whole book, but they can be summarized as follows:

» **Plant** (PL): very creative, the ideas person
» **Resource investigator** (RI): extrovert, good at making outside contacts and developing ideas
» **Monitor/Evaluator** (ME): shrewd and prudent, analytical
» **Shaper** (SH): dynamic and challenging
» **Coordinator** (CO): respected, mature and good at ensuring that talents are used effectively
» **Implementer** (IMP): practical, loyal and task-orientated
» **Completer/Finisher** (CF): meticulous, with great attention to detail
» **Team-worker** (TW): caring and very person-oriented
» **Specialist** (SP): high technical skill, prime loyalties are professional not organizational.

Belbin groups the team roles into three: thinking roles, action roles and social roles, thus covering the three most important attributes of a team – creativity, implementation and social interaction.

For each of the team role strengths listed above, Belbin postulates that there is an allowable weakness, the price that had to be paid for each strength. These are

» **Plant**: weak in communicating with and managing ordinary people
» **Resource investigator**: easily bored after the initial enthusiasm has passed
» **Monitor/Evaluator**: lacks drive and ability to inspire others
» **Shaper**: prone to provocation and bursts of temper
» **Coordinator**: not necessarily the most clever or creative member of the group
» **Implementer**: inflexible and slow to respond to new opportunities
» **Completer/Finisher**: inclined to worry and reluctant to delegate
» **Team-worker**: indecisive in crunch situations
» **Specialist**: contributes on only a narrow front.

It is dangerous to regard the allowable weaknesses as areas to be removed; to do so might also involve losing the underlying strength. The weaknesses need to be understood and managed.

All those who have written on team-work have stressed the need for a balance or blend of team members, and this also applies to the management of diversity. By using diverse rather than similar individuals to make up teams, Belbin has demonstrated that such a team tends to be more successful, provided that the differences and allowable weaknesses are well managed. All forms of diversity can be complementary if managed well: it is not diversity that should be avoided, but its mismanagement.

DISCRIMINATION AND PREJUDICE

Discrimination is the result of the actions of someone who is prejudiced. Most jurisdictions in the developed world have legislation in place dealing with discrimination on the grounds of sex or race. The US has also age discrimination legislation which provides a degree of protection for older workers.

Governments can legislate to prevent discrimination, and can punish those who discriminate against diversity. They cannot, however, legislate against prejudice. Prejudice can only be removed by understanding, education and working with others in circumstances which will demonstrate that similarities are much greater than differences.

KEY LEARNING POINTS

» Different cultural attributes and approaches will lead to different ways of doing things, depending on the culture.
» No single way of doing something is necessarily better than any other way; it may be just more appropriate in the particular circumstances.
» Diversity, whether in culture, gender or personality, may be used to complement skills, and is therefore both effective and productive if managed properly.
» Equity is becoming more important than equality. Difference is something to be celebrated and used, not decried and ignored.

Managing Diversity

Success Stories

» Coca-Cola – global operations using a diverse workforce
» British Airways – global training for a diverse workforce
» Mitsubishi Heavy Industries – the Boeing 777 passenger doors

This chapter contains three case studies based on organizations that have proved successful in managing diversity. All three products are global, and the three organizations have proved adept not only at managing a diverse workforce but also at marketing and delivering their products to a diverse customer base. All three organizations, **Coca-Cola**, **British Airways** and **Mitsubishi**, operate globally, but in the context of this case study, Mitsubishi is actually subcontracted to Boeing for the manufacturer of the passenger doors for the Boeing 777 jet liner, for which British Airways, together with the US-based United Airlines, was a launch customer.

The case studies are all concerned with different areas of organizational activity and different home bases for the organizations concerned:

» **Coca-Cola**: global operations using a diverse workforce
» **British Airways**: global training for a diverse workforce
» **Mitsubishi**: cultural diversity in the supplier/customer relationship

At the end of each case study, the key insights that the study illustrates are summarized.

CASE 1: COCA-COLA – GLOBAL OPERATIONS USING A DIVERSE WORKFORCE

As Mark Pendergrast states in his book *For God, Country and Coca-Cola* (*see* Chapter 9 for details) Coca-Cola is more than a product, it is a global institution; perhaps it is even an icon of the late-twentieth century.

From its inception in 1885 in Atlanta, Georgia, by the morphine-addicted Dr Pemberton, and its subsequent sale as one of many patent medicines for stomach ailments, Coca-Cola has spanned the globe; it is available in nearly every country and every food outlet in the world.

The first versions of the drink may have been addictive, in the truest sense of the word, containing, as has been claimed, small amounts of cocaine (Pendergrast pp 88–9), although this has been denied by the company. It must be stressed that, since 1903, analysis has shown that Coca-Cola has contained no cocaine whatsoever. In the late nineteenth century, cocaine was not recognized as the highly dangerous drug it is known to be today. Sir Arthur Conan Doyle's famous fictional detective Sherlock Holmes was an addict, according to clues in many of books, and contemporary readers of the stories accepted his addiction without comment.

The world-wide interest in Coca-Cola is such that the company has spent $15 million on an Atlanta Museum dedicated to the product, a museum that receives over three thousand visitors per day during the tourist season.

A drink that had apparent beneficial properties and a good taste, and was inexpensive too, had all the ingredients for success at the end of the nineteenth century. As observed in earlier chapters, immigration was swelling the US population (it rose from 50 million in 1880 to 91 million in 1910) and this provided a ready market for Coca-Cola and its rivals – of which there were many.

By 1895 Coca-Cola had lost its medicinal image and was being marketed using bottles and soda fountains simply as a beverage; by 1900 it was available widely across the United States.

In 1897 the company began to sell outside the US, firstly in Hawaii, Mexico and Canada, then expanding to Cuba in 1899 and to the UK in a small way as early as 1900.

By 1909 the drink was not only being exported from the US, but bottling plants had been set up in Cuba, Hawaii and Puerto Rico. The idea of bottling in the area of consumption has been crucial to the success of Coca-Cola; it allows the local customer to identify the product as being more local than it actually is, since it is known to be produced by local workers. There is a paradox here in that Coca-Cola generates local loyalties but is also quintessentially a product of the US, and thus is identified with US values, and even politics and diplomacy as will be shown later in this section.

The famous shaped bottle was first introduced in 1916.

In 1923, the company deemed it the right time to expand into the European market. A series of bottling franchises were arranged, but unfortunately many of the franchisees failed to ensure the purity of their water supplies, which caused major problems and embarrassment for Coca-Cola, as a number of customers became ill.

Nevertheless, in 1932 the UK's first Coca-Cola plant opened outside London – at the same time as Pepsi-Cola began to become a serious rival. This was ironic, as Coca-Cola had the opportunity to buy Pepsi in 1922, but decided against the purchase.

During World War II, US servicemen took Coca-Cola abroad with them and the company went to great lengths to ensure that supplies of the product reached the troops. In West Germany after the war, Coke, like chocolate, became almost an unofficial currency. In the 1950s, bottling and sales commenced throughout Africa, the West Indies, the Middle East and South America. Tourism was growing and vacationers wanted to see products with which they were familiar. The wording on the label might be in a foreign language, but the logo and its color, the bottle and the contents were all the familiar ones from the US. Coca-Cola did not continue this expansion into the communist sphere of influence, but in the 1960s Pepsi did begin to operate behind the Iron Curtain.

It was not until the Japanese government dropped its import controls in 1960 that Coca-Cola could operate there, but by 1964, Coca-Cola had sponsored the Japanese television coverage of the Tokyo Olympics of that year, and the Japanese market became second only to that of the US, accounting for 18% of corporate profits.

Unfortunately for the Coca-Cola Company, the European cold war, beginning with the Berlin airlift in 1948, saw the product being more and more identified with US policy. In the UK, a Labour Member of Parliament spoke against the company, and in France the left wing fomented violence directed at the US in general, and at Coca-Cola in particular as a symbol of 'US Imperialism'.

By operating local plants and providing employment for local people, Coca-Cola was able to weather these storms, and by 1965, the product was available in the Soviet Union. In 1966, Coca-Cola had refused to franchise its operation in Israel, but eventually bowed to political pressure and set up a plant. Unfortunately, the mid-1960s was a bad time for the peace process in the Middle East, with war erupting between Israel and her Arab neighbors in 1967.

The Arab countries announced a boycott of Coca-Cola unless the company pulled out of Israel. This boycott, costing Coca-Cola $20 million in profits per annum, came into effect in 1968, but was short-lived as in Egypt alone it is believed that it led to 25,000 lay-offs.

In 1971, Coca-Cola became truly a global organization with the famous advertisement, 'I'd like to buy the world a Coke ...' Using thirty young people of all races and colors, the advertisement was sung to the tune 'I'd like to teach the world to sing in perfect harmony ...'

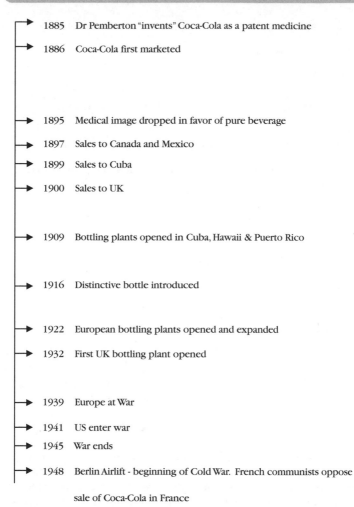

1885   Dr Pemberton "invents" Coca-Cola as a patent medicine

1886   Coca-Cola first marketed

1895   Medical image dropped in favor of pure beverage

1897   Sales to Canada and Mexico

1899   Sales to Cuba

1900   Sales to UK

1909   Bottling plants opened in Cuba, Hawaii & Puerto Rico

1916   Distinctive bottle introduced

1922   European bottling plants opened and expanded

1932   First UK bottling plant opened

1939   Europe at War

1941   US enter war

1945   War ends

1948   Berlin Airlift - beginning of Cold War. French communists oppose

        sale of Coca-Cola in France

Fig. 7.1   Time-line: Coca-Cola.

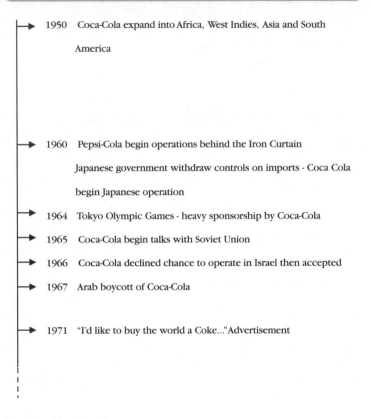

1950	Coca-Cola expand into Africa, West Indies, Asia and South America
1960	Pepsi-Cola begin operations behind the Iron Curtain
	Japanese government withdraw controls on imports - Coca Cola begin Japanese operation
1964	Tokyo Olympic Games - heavy sponsorship by Coca-Cola
1965	Coca-Cola begin talks with Soviet Union
1966	Coca-Cola declined chance to operate in Israel then accepted
1967	Arab boycott of Coca-Cola
1971	"I'd like to buy the world a Coke..." Advertisement

Fig. 7.1 (*Continued*).

This struck a chord with many young people; it expressed the ideals of peace and love – and all brought about by Coca-Cola! The advertisement was so memorable that in 2000 it was voted sixteenth of the 100 greatest TV advertisements in a UK poll. Interestingly, the advertisement was the first positive use of non-white faces in a UK television advertisement. Like the British Airways 'Global' advertisement of 1989, which used a similar format, with different races coming together, the Coca-Cola advertisement was suitable for showing anywhere – it was all-embracing and culturally neutral; exactly what Coca-Cola had been aiming to be as a global product that belonged to everybody.

KEY INSIGHTS

» Make the product appear local even if it is not, thus engendering local loyalty. Coca-Cola calls this 'thinking globally but acting locally'.

» Be culturally sensitive when setting up new plants and operations.

» Be aware that local politics can intrude into operations however good the product is.

» If the product is global, develop advertising that is culturally neutral.

» Use local resources such as franchising to grow the business and acquire local knowledge.

» Be seen as a local benefactor – for example Coca-Cola paid for Japanese coverage of the Tokyo Olympics. The company is also involved in many other sporting and cultural activities.

CASE 2: BRITISH AIRWAYS – GLOBAL TRAINING FOR A DIVERSE WORKFORCE

British Airways (BA) was created as a nationalized airline by the merger in 1974 of British European Airways (BEA) and the British Overseas Airways Corporation (BOAC), as part of a government rationalization of the UK air transportation industry. BOAC's roots went back to Imperial Airways and its predecessors in 1919. In 1974, the newly-formed BA had over 200 aircraft and over 58,000 staff worldwide.

As a nationalized airline, BA had a reputation for poor service and inflexible attitudes, but the privatization of the airline by the UK government in February 1987 was to change the image of BA. The sale of shares in the airline raised over £900 million for the government. Many of the shares were sold to members of the public as part of the Conservative Prime Minister Margaret Thatcher's concept of a share-owning democracy. BA had been preparing for the privatization for some time, and was determined to become a customer-centered player in the global airline market. The antecedents of BA had provided the airline with an extensive route network, especially in areas where the UK had possessed colonial interests. In a surprise move, within a few months of the privatization BA acquired the major UK independent international carrier British Caledonian, gaining additional routes and further capacity at London's rapidly growing second airport, London Gatwick.

The transformation from a staid nationalized state air carrier to the accepted benchmark company for innovation and service proceeded quickly. BA embarked on a policy of growth by partnerships and franchises, both in the UK and abroad. By 1993, for example, BA held a 31% stake in Air Russia, a subsidiary named British Asia Airways, a considerable stake in Brymon European (a UK-based regional operator), a 49% stake in Deutsche BA in Germany, plus links with a number of other European and US carriers. These partnerships and alliances have been a major trend in the airline industry in recent years.

In order to provide a first-class service, BA has had to manage a diverse staff base across the world. BA employs a considerable number of locally-based staff both on the ground and as cabin crew and flight attendants, usually flying to and from their own countries. One of the features of the BA franchise system has been that all the aircraft fly in BA livery and the franchisee's employees wear BA uniforms: it is an important customer care issue that the service received is identical to the standard BA product wherever in the world it is offered. As that service has been rightly considered amongst the best in the world, the franchisee staff must meet the high standards demanded of BA's own staff.

One of the prerequisites of maintaining high standards, according to the US management guru Tom Peters, is an emphasis on initial training and on continuous professional development (CPD). The world's airlines were disrupted by the Gulf War crises of the early 1990s, but in 1992 BA, which had been running an entry level management/supervisory program entitled Fundamentals of Supervision (FOS), decided to re-open tenders for the program. It chose a consortium from Oxford in the UK to design and develop, in close consultation with the BA training staff in London, a re-launch of the program suitable for staff from any part of the network.

The new FOS program was designed around modules covering the context of management, managing people, finance, law, marketing, and the management of information. Each module was assessed through a formative and summative assignment for which the mark did not count towards the final grade, and an end-of-module assignment for which the mark was used to determine the final result. The qualification at the end of the program was a Certificate in Management Studies (CMS), awarded first by one of the UK awarding bodies, and later, after adjustment, by one of the UK universities.

Each module also included a half-day workshop. Initially workshops were held in London, Newcastle, Manchester (all in the UK) and Berlin for German staff. All participants were divided into cohorts of about twelve students, each cohort having a dedicated academic tutor who delivered the seminars and marked the assignments.

Whilst the consortium put forward the names of suitable tutors, it was BA who interviewed them and made the final decision over their engagement.

An important feature of the program was that it had to be accessible and relevant to any members of staff recommended by their line managers as being suitable for the level of training, no matter what their department or their place and country of work. Over the 1990s, participants included pilots, cabin crew/flight attendants, engineers, check-in staff, administrative staff, medical staff, sales representatives and baggage-handling personnel. The geographic range was huge, from Los Angeles to Tokyo and from Berlin to Sydney, with every continent except Antarctica being represented. This meant that training materials had to be prepared with very great care, as motivational techniques and employment law often differs widely between one region and another. It was also necessary to assess assignments with cultural sensitivity. Much of the seminar time was taken up with an exploration of the balance between the cultural requirements of the particular region and the need to meet the BA culture, especially in respect of customer care standards.

In addition to the workshop seminars, all participants attended a three-day weekend residential period held in the Peak District in Derbyshire in Northern England. One of the objectives of the residential period was to introduce the participants to the team-role theory of Meredith

Belbin, and other team building techniques described in Chapter 6. Working in multi-disciplinary and multi-cultural teams, the participants undertook indoor exercises and discussions, as well as a day out on the Derbyshire moors, where each team had to complete a series of tasks involving map reading, rock climbing, caving and abseiling. All these activities were arranged and supervised by qualified outdoor activity instructors, and the program never suffered any serious accidents.

The residential periods, each attended by three cohorts and their tutors, also served to bring people from diverse and distant parts of the airline together, and one of the major benefits reported by participants was the understanding that developed about other people's jobs, their attitudes, and even their culture. The whole thrust of the FOS program was that the skills and knowledge acquired should be applicable in each participant's work situation, regardless of their grade, department or geographic location.

FOS was just one of the BA training initiatives of the 1990s that had staff flying in to London for training, 'Winning for Customers' was another program that was highly successful and actually involved not only all BA staff members, but the staff of franchisees and major suppliers to the airline.

Programs like these are very expensive, especially with up to 200 participants each year, but there is no doubt that the costs of the training were repaid by the standard of service for which BA quickly became a watchword. Indeed, at a time when other airlines were losing money on a regular basis, BA was consistently profitable, showing how much of an investment a carefully planned and implemented training program can be.

FOS was available to all suitable staff and it soon became very popular. Staff acquired management skills and the confidence to use them, and this transferred into the workplace. There was soon a waiting list for the program, especially from overseas staff.

In 1993, the organization decided to expand the Berlin training operation to include the US, with a cohort operating out of BA's US headquarters in Queens, New York. The first cohort included staff from New York itself, Los Angeles, Miami, Atlanta, Washington DC, and Seattle, and from Toronto in Canada. By flying the tutor out to New York, money and, perhaps more importantly, staff time was saved, and the seminars could be focused more directly on US issues. In time, this operation was further expanded to include not just the US (where it operated out of Miami in order to assist flying in staff from the Caribbean and from South and Central America) but also India, South Africa and Australia. The only FOS requirement for the members of these cohorts to visit the UK was for the residential weekend, which remained the same for every participant.

The FOS program is a good example of how careful planning and flexibility can allow a generic product to be delivered to a very diverse group of employees. The message was the same for all staff, since it reflected the core values of the airline, and those remained the same wherever BA operated, but the manner in which the program was delivered could be tailored to meet local needs. This required considerable study by the tutors and a very close liaison between them, the consortium administrators and BA's own training department, as the sponsors of the program.

One extremely important aspect of the FOS program was the inclusion of a 'graduation ceremony' for which BA arranged for the air fares and accommodation of all graduating participants (the success rate was well over 90%) and their partners, plus the tutors and administrators. Certificates were presented by a senior manager, usually the CEO, which very effectively underlined the importance the airline gave to the program. Nobody who wanted to undertake FOS and was recommended by his or her manager was refused a place; if it was not possible to involve applicants immediately, they were at least put on the waiting list. Despite the inclusion of a residential element that could be somewhat physical, culture, gender and disability were all dealt with in a manner which ensured that all participants and, of course BA, gained the maximum benefit from the program.

KEY INSIGHTS

» The FOS program was a partnership between BA's own training staff and an outside training provider (the Consortium).
» The program was designed to fit in with the values and aspirations of the airline.

1991	End of Gulf War (Desert Storm)
1992	Re-tendering for entry-level management program (FOS), contract awarded to Oxford Consortium. Cohorts in UK and Germany
1993	First US cohort (New York)
1994	Cohorts in UK, US (New York) and India (Delhi)
1995	Australian cohort (Sydney) added, re-write of program to fit in with new BA corporate objectives
1996	US cohort moves from New York to Miami
1997	South African cohort (Johannesburg) added

Fig. 7.2 Time-line: British Airways.

» The issues of job and cultural diversity were allowed for at the very beginning of the program.

» The program was designed so that it could be delivered to discrete overseas cohorts in their own region.

» The tutors on the program needed to acquaint themselves with both the culture and operations of BA and those of the staff.

» The program was open to all – the only requirement was motivation and a recommendation from an applicant's line manager.

» The program not only developed skills, by bringing staff together it promoted an understanding of the role and culture of others.

CASE 3: MITSUBISHI HEAVY INDUSTRIES – THE BOEING 777 PASSENGER DOORS

Mitsubishi Heavy Industries in Japan is an old established firm with a diverse range of manufacturing activities including shipbuilding, motor cars and aircraft.

Before the end of World War II, Mitsubishi built no less than ten models of warplane for the Imperial Japanese Army and Navy, ranging from bombers, floatplanes and fighter planes, including the famous A6M Zero-Sen which provided such a shock to the allies, since it outclassed anything the US and the UK had in the early part of the war in the Pacific.

After the war, Japanese industry had to re-build, and for many years the military capacity of Japan was severely curtailed, and limited to a small self-defense force and coastguard, with equipment supplied by the US. Even before the war, aviation research in Japan was primarily military, and there was no tradition of building commercial passenger aircraft. In 1959, a consortium of Japanese engineering companies which had experience in either airframe or aircraft parts manufacture, including Mitsubishi, came together to design and build the Nihon Aeroplane Manufacturing Company's (NAMC) YS-11 turboprop short-haul passenger and freight aircraft, with seating initially limited to 60 passengers. To date this had been the only Japanese commercial transport, apart from the much smaller Mitsubishi MU-2 executive type turboprop. Mitsubishi has since, however, designed and built the T-2 supersonic fighter-bomber for the Japanese Self-defense Force and Kawasaki has designed a military transport, the C-1.

There is no doubt that Japanese industry has been very keen to become involved in commercial jet manufacture. By 2000, it had become apparent that, as a result of mergers, there were only two major players in the commercial jet market – Boeing (which by then had acquired McDonnell Douglas) in the US and Airbus Industrie in Europe. The competition between the two has been fierce since Airbus Industrie was set up in the late 1960s, and has been described by Matthew Lynn in his book *Birds of Prey – Boeing v Airbus* (1995).

In 1970 there had been a tentative idea of selling the Boeing 737 production line to Japan, probably to a consortium consisting of Mitsubishi, Kawasaki and Fuji, but this sale did not materialize. The idea of selling a complete line of production is not that unusual. Many vehicle manufacturers, including Fiat in Europe, UK manufacturers and Japanese companies, have sold complete production facilities, usually to less developed areas. British Aerospace sold the facilities for producing the successful BAC 1-11 airliner to Romania after UK sales began to decline. It is perhaps as well that Boeing did retain the production of the 737, since after a shaky start it has become the best selling and most widely-used jet airliner ever produced.

Mitsubishi had begun to work closely with Boeing during the design stages of the Boeing 747, and by 1974 was producing parts for the Jumbo Jet, as it was called. By the early 1990s it was producing approximately 15% of the components of the smaller Boeing 767.

In the late 1980s, Boeing began the design work on a new aircraft to fill the gap between the 767, which could carry up to 290 passengers just over 9000 km, and the 747, which could take nearly 500 passengers well past the 10,000 km range. The first model new plane was designed to be in the medium distance, 350–400 passenger category, and be powered by only two engines. Modern fan-jets are so reliable that it is perfectly safe to fit only two, unlike the Boeing 747, which needs four. The 777 would be the first aircraft to receive clearance from its debut to fly long, over-water routes using just two engines, and this would make it more flexible to operate as well as cheaper to buy and run.

Boeing involved potential customers at the very earliest design stages, and as Karl Sabbach, who produced an excellent book on the construction of the 777, *Twenty-first Century Jet*, has pointed out, this was to be a very customer-centered product indeed. The book actually supported a UK Channel 4/US KCTS (a public broadcasting channel) documentary series about the design, building and marketing of a modern jet airliner.

A project such as the building of a modern airliner is probably beyond the capabilities of any single company, and there is an increasing reliance on partnerships and the close involvement of suppliers. The Boeing 777 design teams benefited from computer technology which allowed not only a virtual airliner to be constructed, showing how all the parts would fit together, but also the linking of computers in design departments across the world.

The Japanese economic and industrial miracle after World War II lasted well into the 1990s, with Japanese electrical and motor vehicle manufacturers gaining major penetration of global markets. In the US and the UK they also set up manufacturing plants, which meant that they had to deal with the problems of a workforce that showed considerable diversity compared to the traditional workforce from the Japanese home islands. In the main, the Japanese senior management handled this expansion in a sensitive manner, aware of the possible cultural barriers that might be put up against them. Whilst the concepts of total quality management (TQM) for which Japanese industry became renowned for were in fact imported from the US after 1945, Japanese companies had become known both for their high standards and for a loyal workforce which was less prone to industrial action than many of their competitors operating in countries where the Japanese were now setting up plants.

Whilst it was clear that the Japanese would have liked to have been full partners in the 777 project, Boeing was happier with a subcontractor relationship. One of the issues around partnerships and alliances is the guarding of proprietary information and Boeing guards its accumulated knowledge and experience very carefully. Two other books that might interest the reader, and which also analyze the complex builder/sub-contractor relationships within the aircraft construction industry, are Clive Irving's study of the development of the Boeing 747 (*Wide-Body*) and Paul Eddy, Elaine Potter and Bruce Page's *Destination Disaster*, which tells the story of the DC10 and the other first-generation wide-bodied commercial jets. Like *Twenty-first Century Jet*, all of these books are written in a non-technical manner and provide many useful insights. Full details of the books are given in Chapter 9.

Mitsubishi was contracted to manufacture the passenger doors for the 777. Doors are not only a critical operational item for a modern aircraft, they are also vital to safety, as they need to withstand the pressurization forces that are applied in order to provide passengers with ground-level air pressure in the ultra-thin atmosphere at 35,000 ft. It was the loss of a rear cargo door due to a design fault and a rectification failure that led to the loss of 346 lives outside Paris in 1974, as the depressurization collapsed the floor and severed many of the control cables and hydraulics in a Turkish Airlines DC10. Mitsubishi has become renowned for the quality of its doors and is now building the rear cargo doors for the European Airbus Industrie A330/A340 series of long-range jet airliners.

The size of the 777 project was such that it was not just Mitsubishi which was working with Boeing. Much of the aircraft was made both across and outside the US, and then transported to Washington State (Boeing's headquarters is in the Seattle area). Table 7.1 shows just how diverse the spread of the manufacturing program was.

Table 7.1

Component	Where built
Outboard flaps	Italy
Passenger doors	Japan
In-spar ribs	Japan
Elevators	Australia
Rudder	Australia
Engines (for first aircraft)	East Hartford, Connecticut
Automated Spar Assembly	Wisconsin
Some fuselage sections	Japan
Fuel gauges	UK
Nose	Kansas
Entertainment system	UK

Japanese companies are in fact responsible for around 20% of the Boeing 777.

The Boeing 777 benefited from the presence of airline representatives from the very earliest stages of the project and the setting up of design-and-build teams (DBTs) for each set of components. For the passenger doors, the team involved both Boeing and Mitsubishi staff working together, often linked by computers (Boeing uses a sophisticated design tool known as CATIA [Computer-graphics Aided Three-dimensional Interactive Application] to create a virtual aircraft) and video equipment. The design of the doors is complex because of the mechanisms needed to ensure smooth but safe operation, and the fact that each pair of door is slightly different to the others (there are four pairs of passenger doors on a 777) because of the contours of the airframe. Aircraft engineers dislike doors and windows as these mean cut-outs in the metal, and these are where stresses can be very dangerous. It was at a cut-out that the problems which led to the loss of two Comet airliners and the grounding of the whole fleet occurred in the early 1950s, with a consequential devastating effect on the UK aircraft industry.

Tom Gaffney, the leader of the passenger door DBT, spent a great deal of time in Japan, and there were Mitsubishi staff stationed in the Boeing headquarters in Seattle. In fact 25% of Gaffney's engineers were from Mitsubishi, which made for an interesting, diverse team, especially as specialists from Japan would join the team on temporary attachment for specific issues.

As happens in such projects, sooner or later there is likely to be a problem. In the case of the 777 passenger doors, there were delays to the doors. In Japanese society (and in the East, society and work are much more closely linked than in the West – *see* Chapter 6), the manner in which a rebuke is delivered can be very important, since it may cause the recipient to lose face. The emphasis given to the correct degree of respect for individuals within the hierarchy is very important in Japan. In the US an executive could possibly blow off steam in a discussion, apologize, and then the meeting would move on. Such behavior would be highly offensive in a meeting with Japanese colleagues. The relationship between Boeing and Mitsubishi was such that both sides had taken the care to understand the cultural back-grounds of the other. Boeing executives were able to express their concerns with sufficient force to get the point across, but with enough tact to remain polite. Those who manage diverse teams should always bear in mind the importance of a balanced approach.

Boeing has used the same approach with its other Japanese suppliers when there has been a problem, and the sensitivity they have shown has been rewarded by ever-closer relationships and a by high degree of commitment to the project.

The importance of such partnerships cannot be over-stressed. Japanese companies had put up about 10% of the start-up cost of $3 billion required for the 777. Whilst it is clear that the Japanese would have liked a 25% equity stake in the project, their outlay was still large enough to make them important players in the 777 story.

→ 1970s - abortive idea of selling Boeing 737 plant to Japan

→ 1980   Mitsubishi commence work on door for Boeing 767

→ 1988   Boeing begin preliminary discussions with airlines regarding a new

aircraft

→ 1989 Preliminary design of the aircraft, now the Boeing 777, agreed

→ 1992 Major design work on passenger doors

→ 1993 Manufacturing of doors in progress in Japan - delays are

experienced

→ 1994 April 9 - roll out of first aircraft - Boeing have 147 firm orders and

108 options

12 June - first flight

→ 1995 15 May - United Airlines pay Boeing $100 million for their first

aircraft and take delivery

30 May FAA (Federal Aviation Authority) clear the 777 for ETOPS

(Extended Twin-engine Operations) the first commercial jet to be so

rated prior to introduction to service

Fig. 7.3   Time-line: Mitsubishi Heavy Industries.

7 June - first commercial flight of 777, London - Washington DC

(united Airlines)

October - first British Airways Aircraft delivered

→ 1998   Production of a new aircraft every 3 to 4 days

Fig. 7.3   (*Continued*).

The doors were delivered to specification, to budget and on time, and on June 7, 1995, a United Airlines Boeing 777 flew from London's Heathrow Airport to Washington DC, carrying the first paying passengers. United's aircraft were quickly followed into service by those of the other launch customer – British Airways.

The Mitsubishi/Boeing relationship is a small example of how a diverse team, linked by computer and, more importantly, by commitment can overcome cultural diversity to build a world-beating product.

KEY INSIGHTS

» Modern projects are so large that they are beyond a single organization, so diversity is inevitable
» Tact and sensitivity are vital when dealing with diversity
» Properly managed, even a culturally and geographically diverse team can work together to produce excellent results
» Respect and understanding grow over time, and may not be apparent initially
» Technology can aid the management of diversity by linking people together over great distances if necessary.

Key Concepts and Thinkers in Managing Diversity

» A glossary of terms
» Key thinkers

"**Myth**: conflict between groups can be eliminated.
"**Reality**: Employees will always make negative comparisons between their own and other groups. The roots of potential conflict are always present."

Nigel Nicholson – Managing the Human Animal

If we take Nicholson's comment to its ultimate conclusion, it may well be that if diversity did not exist we would need to invent it. As social animals with our origins within a tribal configuration, we actually need diversity in order to function in the correct psychological manner.

The management of diversity is not a subject that can be considered on its own, but rather one that contains ideas from the disciplines of management, psychology and anthropology, What follows is a glossary containing a few of the more commonly-used terms associated with the management of diversity, as well as a more in-depth consideration of some of the key concepts and thinkers on the subject.

A GLOSSARY OF TERMS USED IN MANAGING DIVERSITY

Achievement – in cultural terms, an achievement culture is one that places more emphasis on what a person has done than on his or her family or educational background. The US is an example of an achievement culture (*see* also *Ascription*).

Ascription – in contrast to an achievement culture, an ascription culture puts great emphasis on background and on where a person was educated. Many aspects of Indian culture tend towards ascription.

Collectivism – in a collectivist culture, emphasis is placed first on the group and on the good of society; less emphasis is placed on the individual (*see* also *Individualism*).

Contingency theory – a theory of management much used in contemporary management literature to reflect the belief that there is no single right method of structuring and managing a modern organization, but that the management methods used should be contingent on the situation at each particular time and place.

Culture – the values, attitudes, and beliefs ascribed to and accepted by a group, nation or organization. In effect, 'The way we do things around here'.

Diffuse – in a diffuse culture, the differentiation between work, home and the rest of society is much less marked than in a specific culture (*see* also *Specific*).

DINKY – a social phenomenon occurring towards the end of the twentieth century, standing for 'double income, no kids yet'. DINKYs are young couples who have made a decision to defer starting a family and to concentrate on their careers instead. DINKYs usually possess more disposable income than couples with families.

Discrimination – actions that reflect prejudices by treating one person or group of people less well than another. Whilst prejudice is concerned with beliefs, discrimination manifests itself in conscious or unconscious negative actions.

Diversity – the differences between groups and individuals. In the case of the management of diversity, the similarities between humans are always far greater than their differences. Diversity is the rich mix of customs, beliefs, language and experiences.

Emotional – an emotional culture is one in which it is permissible to show feelings, even in the work situation (*see* also *Neutral*).

Glass ceiling – the invisible barrier that many societies erect, consciously or unconsciously, to hinder the progress of women within career structures.

Globalization – the trend towards organizations which operate in a world-wide manner, offering similar products and services but often using different brand names in different places.

Harmonic tension – the tensions that actually work together positively in a group where the team roles are well balanced and create a synergy (*see* also *Synergy* and *Team roles*)

Home working – a trend accelerated by the use of information and communications technology, enabling people to work from home on complex tasks, with no need to visit an organization's premises.

Homogenous work force – a work force comprising a group showing little diversity.

Hygiene factors – factors which, if absent, lead to dissatisfaction with work, but when present do not actually motivate workers (*see* also *Motivators*).

Individualism – a culture which puts the individual's rights at the forefront of the value system, as opposed to the group approach of a collectivist culture (*see* also *Collectivism*).

Motivators – factors which, when present in the workplace, increase motivation (*see* also *Hygiene factors*).

Neutral – a culture in which shows of emotion are not valued in the workplace (*see* also *Emotional*).

Particularism – a culture where rules are not applied universally, but may differ according to the situation (*see* also *Universalism*).

Personalities – the behavioral traits that distinguish one individual from another.

Prejudice – negative beliefs about a particular individual or group of individuals. Prejudice is often irrational and may lead to discrimination (*see* also *Discrimination*).

Primates – the animal group to which humans belong. Primates are highly intelligent mammals with stereoscopic and color vision, and are able to rotate the radius over the ulna in the forearm and oppose the thumb and fingers, making them highly dextrous.

Scientific management – an early twentieth century concept proposed by F.W. Taylor in the US, based on the idea that work could be measured and rates set for each job based on the measurements. The concept assumes that money is the main motivator for work.

Social animals – animals that live in defined social groups such as man, elephants, bees, wolves.

Specific – a culture in which work and home are clearly separate (*see* also *Diffuse*).

Synergy – a phenomenon where the whole is greater than the sum of the parts. A team of five working in synergy can often produce the output of six.

Team roles – the tendency of individuals to behave in a certain way when working within a team (*see* also *Team role theory*).

Team role theory – a concept pioneered by Meredith Belbin in the UK, proposing that a successful team contains individuals who take up specific team roles, based on personality, in addition to their functional work roles.

Universalism – a culture in which rules are applied to all members of the society with little variation for circumstances. (*see* also *Particularism*).

KEY THINKERS IN MANAGING DIVERSITY

All of the books referred to in this section are listed fully in Chapter 9.

Belbin, Meredith

Working in the UK from the 1980s onwards, Meredith Belbin proposed the concept of team roles and used it to study successful and unsuccessful teams. His work has since spread throughout the world and is used in team building and as a recruitment aid by many organizations. The nine team roles that Belbin proposed need to be present in a team to ensure the necessary balance and synergy for effective performance. Thus diversity in team membership is a positive factor and should be welcomed. Individuals can be tested for their preferred team roles using a questionnaire and the *Interplace*® software developed by Belbin Associates. Belbin's later work has linked the team role theory to organizational design.

There are regular *Interplace*® user conferences, and a newsletter indicating how the software is used in the field by organizations that have adopted it.

One of the most important aspects of Belbin's work on the management of diversity is that it provides a mechanism for describing diverse members of a team, using a language which is neither prejudicial, insulting, or threatening to the individual.

Highlights
Books:

» *Management Teams – Why they Succeed or Fail* (1981)
» *Team Roles at Work* (1993)
» *The Coming Shape of Organization* (1996).

Other:

» *Interplace*® software for team role profiling (detailed in Chapter 9).

Davidson, Marilyn J.

A writer on the glass ceiling effect on women's careers, Davidson has worked with others (Gary L. Cooper & Kamlesh Bahl) on the position of women at work, including those from racial minorities.

In their book *The Black and Ethnic Minority Woman Manager* (1977), Davidson and Bahl produced one of the few UK works on the subject.

Shattering the Glass Ceiling (1992) was one of the earliest works to inform management about the glass ceiling effect and its demotivational impact on women managers.

Davidson is also one of the editors of *Women in Management – Current Research Issues* series that covers areas of particular interest to women managers and which takes a global perspective on the issues.

With Gary L. Cooper she has edited *European Women in Business and Management* (1993), which considers the past, present, and future position of women managers in the European Union member states.

Highlights

Books:

» *Shattering the Glass Ceiling* (with G. Cooper) (1992)
» *European Women in Business and Management* (with G. Cooper) (1993)
» *The Black and Ethnic Minority Woman Manager* (with K. Bahl) (1997)
» *Women in Management – Current Research Issues* (2000).

Handy, Charles

For many years a professor at the London Business School, Charles Handy is now an independent writer and broadcaster, describing himself as a social philosopher. His work with Shell and at the Sloan School of Management at the Massachusetts Institute of Technology, where he gained an MBA, fired his fascination with organizations and how they work.

Handy's main concern is the implication for society, and for individuals, of the dramatic changes which technology and economics are bringing to the workplace and to all our lives. His book *The Empty Raincoat* (published as *The Age of Paradox* in the US) is a sequel to his earlier best-selling *The Age of Unreason*, which first explored these changes, and was named by both *Fortune* and *Business Week* as one of the ten best business books of 1995. His books, which include the popular *Gods of Management* (1992) as well as the standard textbook *Understanding Organizations*, have sold over a million copies around the world. In both of these books Handy expounded his model of corporate cultures and how they interact, adding considerably to the body of knowledge on the subject of managing diversity, in these cases diversity within and between organizations. *The Empty Raincoat/Age of Paradox* was awarded the J.S.K. Accord Prize for the Best Business Book of the Year in 1994. *Beyond Certainty*, a collection of articles and essays, was published in 1995 (1996 in the US), as was *Waiting for the Mountain to Move*, a collection of his radio 'Thoughts' gathered over ten years. His book *The Hungry Spirit*, in which he airs doubts about some of the consequences of free market capitalism and questions whether material success can ever provide the true meaning of life, was published in the UK in September 1997 and in the US in January 1998.

Highlights

Books:

- » *Understanding Organizations* (1976)
- » *The Gods of Management* (1978)
- » *The Empty Raincoat* (UK), *The Age of Paradox* (US) (1995)
- » *The Age of Unreason* (1997)
- » *Beyond Certainty* (1996)
- » *The New Alchemists* (1999).

Articles:

- » *Harvard Business Review*, "Balancing Corporate Power: A New Federalist Paper" (1992)

» *Harvard Business Review*, "Trust and the Virtual Organization" (1995).

Harris, Philip & Moran, Robert

Harris and Moran are two US writers who have looked at techniques of management across cultural diversity and at the issues surrounding gender and other diversity factors. Their very well-written work takes a US perspective and provides examples of the differences between other cultures and that of the US. Their comments on the UK are particularly interesting, and highlight some of the more subtle differences between two apparently closely-related cultures. They have also stressed the importance of business leaders developing a global approach to modern business leadership.

Highlights

Books:

» *Developing the Global Organization* (with W.G. Stripp) (1993)
» *Managing Cultural Differences* (1979; fifth edition, 2000).

Lewis, Richard D.

Richard Lewis is an authority on the management of cultural diversity difference. He is the founder of the magazine Cross Culture and in addition to speaking over twelve languages he has worked with a large number of major multi-national organizations. Lewis makes the point that mutual understanding and sensitivity lie at the heart of managing across cultures. In both *When Cultures Collide* and *Cross-Cultural Communications – A visual approach*, Lewis stresses the importance of ensuring that the communications process is as robust as possible. The same words and phrases can mean different things in different cultures but (although there are still some differences) non-verbal, visual communications can often convey true meanings better than verbal ones. *Cross-Cultural Communications* also contains visual materials from Lewis's seminars and this makes the book a very useful resource for training.

Lewis provides useful ideas on the classifying of cultures and the traits and tendencies of members of particular cultures. On the very practical side he provides advice on behavior for managers, dealing with inter-cultural issues and the management of diversity.

Having developed a model for cultural analysis, Lewis has produced two PC-based packages on the subject. The first, *Cross-Cultural Assessor*, is a tool for cross-cultural analysis applicable to individuals and across an organization. The second, *Gulliver*, provides both cross-cultural training and a database to set up 'what if' scenarios.

Richard D. Lewis Communications and the associated Institute of Cross-Cultural Communication (both based in the UK but operating globally) also produce a Cross-Cultural Letter to International Managers. This is issued ten times a year and available on subscription. Lewis and his associates cover many areas in this journal; some of the topics discussed in recent editions include:

1 Cultural Factors in International Negotiation and Circular Thinking
2 Life within Horizons and Cultural Factors in International Negotiation
3 The Language of Management and Cultural Factors in International Negotiation
4 Concepts of Time
5 Anglo-Saxons: World's Worst or Best Linguists?
6 Germans: Appearance and Reality
7 Language and Thought
8 The Maverick French
9 The Use of Silence in Business
10 The Russians are Coming
11 National Listening Habits
12 The World through Spanish Eyes
13 Manners & Mannerisms.

Highlights
Books:

» *When Cultures Collide* (2000)
» *Cross-Cultural Communications – A visual approach* (1999)

Computer programs:

» *Cross-Cultural Assessor* a multimedia product designed to assist individuals and organizations in measuring, building and managing cross-cultural skills and characteristics.

» *Gulliver* a computer-based training product – delivered either on-line or via CD-ROM. A joint venture between Richard Lewis and PriceWaterhouseCoopers. The purpose of *Gulliver* is to help people involved in international business to perform successfully across cultures.

Nicholson, Nigel

Nigel Nicholson is a psychologist who has linked managerial concepts to those from evolutionary development. His work has won critical acclaim from managerial specialists and psychologists alike. Exploring the psychology of human groups and clans he has been able to provide useful insights into the management of diversity, particularly racial or gender diversity.

Nicholson's work is easy to read and yet highly informative and takes managerial studies into behavioral psychology in a masterful manner.

Highlights

Books:

» *Managing the Human Animal* (2000)

Stith, Anthony

Author of *Breaking the Glass Ceiling – Sexism and Racism in Corporate America*, and *How to Build a Career in the New Economy: A Guide for Minorities and Women*, Stith has been one of a number of writers who have exposed the irrationality of the bar to women and minorities progressing in organizations – the glass ceiling.

Stith comments that the glass ceiling is a phrase used to describe artificial barriers based on attitudinal or organizational biases which prevent qualified minorities and women from not only advancing upward into middle and senior level positions, but into entry and lower level positions as well. This phenomenon adversely affects more than half of US society, and is equally damaging in most western cultures, and yet society has constantly failed to address it adequately.

Stith says that he wrote the *Breaking the Glass Ceiling* as a vehicle to dismantle discriminatory beliefs and practices in today's workforce, and to provide effective tools that can help employees, employers and institutions to develop awareness, sensitivity and a commitment to resolve this issues. His work is not about being anti-gender, anti-white or anti-any race. It is about being anti-discrimination.

His books were written with the knowledge that it is impossible to force others to discard prejudicial beliefs. Instead he uses a more sensible approach that makes offenders willingly stop discriminatory practices. This is accomplished by demonstrating that it is in their best interests to change, and pointing out how they will reap benefits by eliminating discrimination.

Stith believes that the glass ceiling is one of the greatest challenges US and other societies face. It is a plague upon society and will only be vanquished when all minorities, women and non-minorities, institutions and businesses become active participants in eliminating the problem. This book can be a blueprint to a successful career for anyone who involved in management. As Stith says, "Employers and institutions will also learn to achieve and maintain success by properly utilizing and motivating their most important assest – their entire workforce, regardless of race and gender."

Highlights

Books:

» *Breaking the Glass Ceiling – Sexism and Racism in Corporate America* (1998)
» *How to Build a Career in the New Economy: A Guide for Minorities and Women* (1999).

Trompenaars, Fons

Working originally in the Netherlands for Royal Dutch Shell, Fons Trompenaars has been one of the most influential writers on the management of cultural diversity. Shell is a global organization with considerable experience in managing diversity, and Trompenaars set out to put these experiences into a conceptual framework that could be transferred to other organizations. It is hard to find work on cultural diversity in the work-place that does not cite Trompenaars.

His first book, *Riding the Waves of Culture – understanding cultural diversity in business*, was published in 1993 and was purchased in large quantities by organizations such as British Airways, where it was required reading for the tutors employed on the management program detailed in the case study in Chapter 7. The book not only provided a contextual framework, it also provided concrete examples of the differing cultural norms that managers were likely to encounter, and strategies for dealing with them in a sensitive and effective manner.

In association with Charles Hampden-Turner, Trompenaars has looked in more detail at the competencies required for cross-cultural management (in *Building Cross-cultural Competence*) and at the requirements for twenty-first century business leaders in a more global-ized environment (in *21 Leaders for the 21st Century*) as well as giving a detailed examination of social, cultural and economic differences between Asia and the West (in *Mastering the Infinite Game*).

The cultural attributes considered in Chapter 6 (attitude to time, universal vs. particular, individualism vs. collectivism, emotional vs. neutral, specific vs. diffuse, achievement vs. ascription, and attitudes to the environment) were all first described by Trompenaars, with specific examples of each related to a series of different cultures, to show how a similar scenario may well be dealt with in very varying ways.

Fons Trompenaars is recommended reading for all those dealing with cultural diversity within the work-place; he blends practical advice with a useful conceptual framework.

Highlights

Books:

» *Riding the Waves of Culture* (1997)
» *Mastering the Infinite Game* (with C. Hampden-Turner) (1997)
» *Building Cross-Cultural Competence* (with C. Hampden-Turner) (2000)
» *21 Leaders for the 21st Century* (with C. Hampden-Turner) (2001)

Wirth, Linda

Linda Wirth is another of the writers who have examined the glass ceiling. Her book *Breaking Through the Glass Ceiling* deals specifi-cally with gender issues and is published by the International Labor

Organization (ILO), showing the global nature of the issue. Wirth comments that women around the world have achieved higher levels of education than ever before and today represent more than 40 per cent of the global workforce. Yet their share of management positions remains low, with just a tiny proportion succeeding in breaking through the glass ceiling.

Wirth's study reviews the changing position of women in the labor market and in professional and managerial work. It examines the obstacles to women's career development and the action taken to improve their opportunities and promote gender equality. The 2000 edition has been revised and updated. It discusses the earnings gap between men and women, as well as the occupational segregation that exists in management. It also examines the situation of women managers in the area of public service as well as the financial, business and banking sectors, and provides valuable figures and statistical information. It addresses the hurdles that women encounter in the recruitment and promotion process, and offers career-building strategies such as mentoring, networking and career tracking.

Highlights

Book:

» *Breaking Through the Glass Ceiling* (2000).

Resources for Managing Diversity

- » Books
- » Journals
- » Software
- » Web sites

BOOKS ON CULTURE AND DIVERSITY

Belbin, M. R. (1981) *Management Teams – Why they Succeed or Fail*, Heinemann, Oxford.

Belbin, M. R. (1993) *Team Roles at Work*, Butterworth Heinemann, Oxford.

Belbin, M. R. (1996) *The Coming Shape of Organization*, Butterworth Heinemann, Oxford.

Davidson, M. & Bahl, K. (1997) *The Black and Ethnic Minority Woman Manager*, Paul Chapman, London.

Davidson, M.& Cooper, G. (1992) *Shattering the Glass Ceiling*, Paul Chapman, London.

Davidson, M. & Cooper, G, (1993) *European Women in Business and Management*, Paul Chapman, London.

Davidson, M. & Burke, R. J. (eds) (2000), *Women in Management – Current Research Issues vol 2, 2000*, Sage, London.

Gray, J. (1992) *Men are from Mars, Women are from Venus*, Harper-Collins, New York.

Handy, C. (1976) *Understanding Organizations*, Penguin, London.

Handy, C. (1978) *Gods of Management*, Souvenir Press, London.

Handy, C. (1995) *The Age of Unreason*, Arrow, London.

Handy, C. (1995) *The Empty Raincoat* (UK) / *Age of Paradox* (US); Arrow, London (UK), Harvard Business School, Cambridge (Ma) (US).

Handy, C. (1996) *Beyond Certainty*, Harvard Business School, Cambridge (Ma).

Handy, C. & Handy, E. (1999) *The New Alchemists*, Hutchinson, London.

Handy, C. (2000) *21 Ideas for Managers*, Jossey-Bass, San Francisco.

Harris, P. R. & Moran, R. T. (2000) *Managing Cultural Differences*, Gulf Publishing Co., Houston.

Hastings, C., Bixby, P. & Chaudhry-Lawton, R. (1994) *Superteams*, HarperCollins, London.

Herzberg, F. (1962) *Work and the Nature of Man*, World Publishing, New York.

Huntingdon, S. (1996) *The Clash of Civilizations and the Remaking of World Order*, Simon and Shuster, New York.

Lewis, R. D. (2000) *When Cultures Collide*, Nicholas Brealey, London.

Lewis, R. D. (1999) *Cross Cultural Communications – A Visual Approach*, Transcreen, London.

Moran, R. T. & Harris, P. R. (2000) *Managing Cultural Differences*, Gulf Publishing Co., Houston.

Moran, R. T., Harris, P. R. & Stripp, W. G. *Developing the Global Organization – Strategies for Human Resource Professionals*, Gulf Publishing Co., Houston.

Nicolson, N. (2000) *Managing the Human Animal*, Crown, New York.

Nicolson, N. & Nicholson, J. (2000), *A1*, Collins, London.

Pettinger, R. (1998) *The European Social Charter*, Kogan Page, London.

Stith, A. (1998) *Breaking the Glass Ceiling – Sexism and Racism in Corporate America*, Warwick Publishing, New York.

Stith, A. (1999) *How to Build a Career in the New Economy: A Guide for Minorities and Women*, Warwick Publishing, New York.

Taylor, F. W. (1911). *Principles of Scientific Management*, Harper, New York.

Trompenaars, F. (1993) *Riding the Waves of Culture*, Economist Books, London.

Trompenaars, F. & Hampden-Turner, C. (1997), *Mastering the Infinite Game*, Capstone, Oxford.

Trompenaars, F. & Hampden-Turner, C. (2000) *Building Cross-Cultural Competence*, John Wiley & Sons, London.

Trompenaars, F. & Hampden-Turner, C. (2001) *21 Leaders for the 21st Century*, Capstone, Oxford.

Wirth, L. (2000) *Breaking through the Glass Ceiling*, International Labor Organization, Geneva.

BOOKS WITH DETAIL ON THE CASES COVERED IN CHAPTER 7

For information about Coca-Cola:

Pendergrast, M. (2000) *For God, Country and Coca-Cola*, Orion, London.

For information about British Airways and the airline industry:

Hanlon, P. (1999) *Global Airlines*, 2nd edn, Butterworth Heinemann, Oxford.

Marriot, L. (2000) *British Airways*, Ian Allan, Shepperton.

For information about Boeing, Mitsubishi and commercial aircraft design and manufacture:

Eddy, P., Potter, E. & Page, B. (1976) *Destination Disaster*, Hart-Davis, London.
Irving, C. (1993) *Wide Body, the Making of the Boeing 747*, Hodder & Stoughton, London.
Sabbach, K. (1995) *21st Century Jet – the Making of the Boeing 777*, Macmillan, Basingstoke.

JOURNALS

Cross Cultural Letter to International Managers, ten edns per year, Richard Lewis Publications, www.crossculture.com

Harvard Business Review, leading business and management resource with contributions by the leading names in business and management. Ten edns per year, available world-wide and by subscription, www.hbsp.harvard.edu/products/hbr

HR Magazine, a Human Resource magazine covering a wide range of issues, Society for Human Resource Management, Alexandria (Va), www.shrm.org

Human Resource Management International Digest, A digest of useful HR articles from many international sources, seven edns per year, subscription only, www.mcb.co.uk/hrmid/html

International Journal of Human Resource Management, concerned with strategic human resource management and future international trends. Eight edns per year, also by subscription, Routledge, www.tandf.co.uk/journals/routledge

Management Today, often contains useful articles on issues concerned with diversity. Institute of Management in the UK, monthly to members or by subscription, www.inst-mgt.org.uk

People Management, magazine of the UK Chartered Institute of Personnel and Training. Contains articles on all aspects of personnel and training, with especial relevance to the UK. Fortnightly by subscription, www.peoplemanagement.co.uk

SOFTWARE

Interplace®

A software package developed by Belbin Associates in the UK to support the assessment of team roles and to provide a recruitment package to ensure the appointment of the right person to fit into the existing organization. **Interplace** integrates data about people and jobs, data gained through a standardized procedure comprising self-perception exercises, observer assessments, job requirement and observations evaluations. These inputs generate advice from an expert computer system that has been built up over a period of ten years.

As a Human Resource Management System, **Interplace** enables better decisions to be made about people. These better decisions arise from having information based on a broader database of information condensed into a format that is easy to understand and relevant to the issue at hand. **Interplace** focuses on a type of information that is often difficult to obtain and difficult to process, since it relates to the nature of an individual's contribution and potential work. **Interplace** does not incorporate data about a candidate's qualifications and experience, but it does provide an important supplement to such information in facilitating decisions on personnel issues.

Interplace produces individually-tailored reports using four sources of information:

The Self-Perception Inventory (SPI), how the individual sees him or herself in team-role terminology

Observer Assessments, how the individual is seen by at least four other people who know him or her well

Job Requirements, how a line manager (or someone with direct responsibility) sees a job

Job Observations, how those who know the job well see the job.

Interplace integrates self-knowledge with the assessments of others to generate an overall profile to describe a person's actual behavior.

Cross-Cultural Assessor

Developed by Richard D. Lewis, this is a multimedia product designed to assist individuals and organizations in measuring, building and managing cross-cultural skills and characteristics. The program analyzes users' knowledge of world cultures, as well as their personal style and beliefs, through a variety of attractive exercises and questionnaires. It creates a personalized feedback report on individual users, which then details their level of cultural awareness and their adaptability, giving them a picture of how others might see them in cultural terms. It then makes recommendations for developing their cross-cultural skills. The program collects data on groups of individuals to help employers with training, development and international assignment decision.

Gulliver

A computer-based training product, delivered either on-line or via CD-ROM. It is a joint venture between Richard Lewis and PriceWaterhouse Coopers. The purpose of *Gulliver* is to help people involved in international business to perform successfully across cultures. It is particularly aimed at users who have limited time.

Gulliver has two main sections

1 *The Visitor: Introduction to Cross Cultural Communication*. This section provides the user with a thorough introduction to the subject of cross-cultural interaction, covering topics such as human mental programming, life within horizons, categorization of cultures, listening habits, concepts of space and time, language of management, decision-making, and leadership styles.
2 *The Navigator: Solving Specific Issues*. The second section allows the user to specify a particular cross-cultural problem and to receive specific advice to resolve that problem. A huge database of information gives an immediate response and means that virtually all common business situations are covered.

WEB SITES

For information about specific countries and their cultures, use a search engine to search for that country. For specific organizations, search using the organization's name. Sites for journals and other publications are listed under the journal section above.

Useful information can be found at the following Web sites:

www.belbin.com (web site for Meredith Belbin and **Interplace** software)

www.boeing.com (Boeing web site)

www.british-airways.com (British Airways web site)

www.cocacola.com (Coca-Cola web site)

www.crossculture.com (Web site for Richard D. Lewis)

www.edu/gov-res.html (US government information service World Wide Web virtual library and database)

www.europa.eu.int (European Union home page)

www.europa.eu.int/en/comm/eurostat/facts/wwwroot/en/index. htm (European Union statistics)

www.fedworld.gov (Federal World Information Network operated by US government)

www.ilo.org (International Labor Organization)

www.mitsubishi.com (Mitsubishi web site)

www.princesscruises.com (Princess Cruises web site)

www.open.gov.uk (UK public sector information)

www.odci.gov/cia/publications/factbook/index.html (World Fact-book – CIA/USA)

www.statistics.gov.uk (UK Government Office of National Statistics)

www.uhi.ac.uk (University of the Highlands and Islands web site).

Ten Steps to Making Managing Diversity Work

The ten steps to making managing diversity work are:

1 Know the culture of the organization
2 Find out about the culture of the area, region or country
3 3: Understand the culture of the individual or group of employees
4 Understand the nature of the business
5 Understand yourself
6 Be sensitive
7 Encourage diversity
8 Equity/equality
9 Educate against prejudice
10 Act against discrimination.

In the modern world, even the smallest organization will be dealing with diversity. Diversity of staff, diversity of suppliers and diversity of customers is now the norm in any business. From the smallest gas station to an international oil company, from a small car lot to an international manufacturer, from a real estate agent to a construction conglomerate, from a wayside diner to a global burger chain, managing an organization means managing diversity.

The organizations, large or small, that will be successful in the fast-changing commercial, economic and political world of the twenty-first century will be those that can use diversity to their advantage, that can see in diversity an opportunity and not a threat.

This book has provided a guide to the issues involved in managing diversity, whether it is in a small, diverse team or in a workforce spread across the globe. This chapter offers ten steps to assist organizations and individuals in the process of managing diversity. It might be thought that the steps are just common sense. That is half right. They do make sense, but unfortunately they are not always a common phenomenon when common sense is most needed.

The ten steps are followed by ten Frequently Asked Questions (FAQs) which refer back to material in the first nine chapters of the book.

The ten steps are actions that need to be carried out in parallel. The exact order and the degree of priority given to them will, like contingency theory described in Chapter 3, depend on the circum-stances of each situation. One of the key skills of management is the ability to analyze a situation and decide on the appropriate action. Information to assist the analytical process can be found in the references in Chapter 9 and on the Internet. It is not possible, as F.W. Taylor tried (*see* Chapter 3), to lay down a set of universal mechanical rules for management. The way diversity is managed in one organization may be very different from that in another. The issues that need to be considered, and thus the first four steps, are an analysis of:

» The culture of the organization
» The culture of the area, region or country
» The culture of the individual or group of employees
» The nature of the business.

KNOW THE CULTURE OF THE ORGANIZATION

Handy's work on organizational cultures was introduced in Chapters 6 and 8 and every manager should have considered the culture of his or her own organization, and the impact that this might have on other organizations and individuals who may operate to a different set of norms. There is little point in analyzing the outside world unless a manager has a very clear idea of how his or her own organization works and, equally critically, why it works in that way. Why do certain organizations have complex rules and others are more laid back? The answer will lie at the cultural level and may well be linked to the beliefs and philosophies of the organization's founder.

FIND OUT ABOUT THE CULTURE OF THE AREA, REGION OR COUNTRY

The importance of the culture of the outside environment, especially where the organization is moving into a new area, was stressed in Chapter 3 and in the work of Trompenaars, Lewis and Harris & Moran (Chapters 6 and 8) and has been a theme throughout this book.

All managers working in a new region must equip themselves with a knowledge of the cultural and social attitudes of that area.

UNDERSTAND THE CULTURE OF THE INDIVIDUAL OR GROUP OF EMPLOYEES

The culture of an individual, or of a culturally-similar group of employees, is likely to be composed of factors connected with the culture of their place of origin (whether they were actually born their or not) and the culture of where they live now. Even people not born in a place may be brought up in its cultural traditions; second and third generation citizens of an adopted country can often retain their true native culture far more fiercely that their emigrant ancestors did. However, the longer people live away from what might be called their birth culture, the more the two cultures will become intertwined.

Many people operate within two or even three cultures; a culture at home, a culture when they are out socially, and yet a third at work. This only presents problems when aspects of one culture conflict with those of another. This conflict presents a major dilemma – which culture to follow. Someone from a culture where honesty is highly valued may have problems if asked by an employer to mislead a customer (it should not happen, but it does).

One of the most extreme cases of this culture-conflict resulted in the Indian Mutiny of 1857–1859. In 1856, the UK annexed the semi-independent kingdom of Oudh (now part of the state of Uttar Pradesh in India), and the soldiers of that kingdom (known as *sepoys*) were incorporated into the army of the East India Company. The *sepoys* felt that British rule failed to respect their traditions of religion and caste. They resented the British introduction of social changes, the efforts of Christian missionaries to convert them, and the fact that they were forced to serve their new masters in wars outside India. Mounting discontent culminated in open revolt when the East India Company issued new Enfield rifles. To load the rifles, the *sepoys* had to bite off the ends of greased cartridges. Rumors circulated that the cartridges were greased with the fat of cows and pigs, and this outraged both Hindus, who regard cows as sacred, and Muslims, who regard pigs as unclean.

The first mutinous act occurred on May 10, 1857, at Meerut, when 85 *sepoys*, who had been placed in chains for refusing to use the new cartridges, were freed by their comrades. The mutineers killed many of their officers and set out for nearby Delhi, which they captured with the help of the local garrison. Regiments then revolted at Cawnpore, which was captured, and Lucknow, which was besieged. The mutinies, and the British reprisals which followed them, were equally savage. The *sepoys* vastly outnumbered the British soldiers, and the rebellion quickly spread over north and central India, gaining popular support as it went. It was not, however, a national uprising and by 1859 it had been crushed. The East India Company that had ruled India for Britain now found that the government was no longer prepared to allow an individual organization to wield power over a sub-continent, and rule of India passed to the British government.

The consequences of ignoring a cultural tradition were immense and have had a dramatic effect on world history; India became the jewel in the crown of the British Empire before it finally achieved independence and is now, thanks to a blending of cultures, the most populous democracy in the world.

UNDERSTAND THE NATURE OF THE BUSINESS

Different sectors of business have different ways of doing things. Co-operation between competitors may be encouraged or actively discouraged, the amount of credit allowed may differ, working practices may vary widely. All managers should have a good working knowledge of all sectors that interface with their organization. They are likely to meet diverse working practices, some of which may be alien to their own way of doing things. This does not make them wrong, just different. What works in one sector may be totally inappropriate in another.

UNDERSTAND YOURSELF

Imagine a scenario where a three US managers are working with a group of employees in a US-based organization in Brazil. Who is dealing with diversity? The answer, of course, is that both sets of people are. It is all too easy to regard others as different without remembering that they will see you and your colleagues as different. This situation does not just happen to different national groups; it can happen between members of different departments working on the same site.

In order to be sensitive, the next step in this chapter, it is necessary to understand one's own prejudices and feelings. An analysis of them may point out irrationalities that need to be addressed. The more comfortable a person is with himself or herself, the more effectively he or she will be able to manage diversity.

BE SENSITIVE

In the case of the Indian Mutiny described in Step 3, an awareness of cultural attitudes and a little sensitivity from the British officers would have defused the situation at an early stage and many lives on both sides would have been saved. Arrogance and assumed superiority are two great enemies of managing diversity. The belief that one's way of doing things is superior may, in fact, be true or it may not be true at all, but the method by which this belief is communicated is all important. Sensitive handling of diversity and a willingness to listen and take new ideas on board is a critical skill for all managers, especially those who have to manage diversity.

ENCOURAGE DIVERSITY

The work of Meredith Belbin (described in Chapters 6 and 8) on team roles has shown the importance of encouraging diversity. Belbin's research demonstrated that homogenous teams, i.e. those composed of similar personalities, were less successful than those that were diverse. Despite the problems that diversity in teams might cause, correct management of the allowable weaknesses creates a considerable degree of synergy. Whatever the type of diversity, whether it is based on gender, race, culture, personality or anything else, the diverse experiences and ideas can, if managed effectively, produce results that are better than those from a homogenous situation. It is worth remembering that every problem raised by diversity is not only a challenge, it is also an opportunity.

EQUITY/EQUALITY

Chapter 6 raised the difference between equality and equity. Semantically, equality means treating everybody the same whilst equity means providing different experiences but to the same standard and level. Current management practice recognizes diversity and thus stresses equity. Organizations working in a global environment may not be in a position to treat people equally. For instance, wage rates and the cost of living differ widely throughout the world. Giving US-level wages to employees in a country where the cost of living is lower than that in the US, but where wage rates are also lower, would make them relatively better off than their US colleagues.

Equity involves taking local conditions and culture into account. If a large number of staff in a US organization's US plant speak Spanish, should all communication be in English? The answer may well be yes, because the plant deals with outsiders too – suppliers, customers, neighbours, competitors. Customer communications should be in the language used by the customer, but a wise management will recognise that for purely internal use, dual language notices can be employed. In this way everybody's sensitivities will be addressed.

Equality is a simple solution to diversity, whereas equity is more effective but more complex. To ensure equity involves an understanding of the nature of the diversity and a desire to treat people as individuals with their own unique needs.

EDUCATE AGAINST PREJUDICE

Prejudice, however irrational, exists in the mind, and it is not possible to legislate against it. Discrimination (*see* Step 10) can and should be legislated against. Discrimination is prejudice in action.

The way to deal with prejudice is through education. Education is not something only for the young. All people learn throughout their lives. A preparedness to continue learning may well contribute to a longer life. The type of education that combats prejudice involves learning about others and gaining an understanding of the reasons they do things the way they do. Whilst this may take time and effort, it is worth reflecting that one definition of learning is 'a permanent change in behavior'. It is that permanence of knowledge and understanding that can remove prejudice. Managers should take every opportunity to improve both their own knowledge of diversity and the knowledge of those for whom they have managerial responsibility.

ACT AGAINST DISCRIMINATION

Whilst prejudice can only be educated against, discrimination can and should be acted upon. Many jurisdictions have enacted anti-discriminatory legislation as described in Chapter 6. Managers should ensure that no discriminatory practices (even casual comments and humor which can cause offense) are allowed. Part of equity is respect, and discrimination is not only illegal, it is also disrespectful. It is highly demotivating to all parties and thus impacts widely on organizational efficiency. Sensitivity is important. A first offense can provide the initial step in educating against prejudice, but if it is ignored, it is likely to lead to an escalation in inappropriate behavior.

Frequently Asked Questions (FAQs)

Q1: Wouldn't it be easier to treat everybody the same?

A: It is better to know and understand the diversity of people and treat them with equity rather than equality. Equity means treating people to the same standard, but with sensitivity to cultural and other differences. Equity is about fairness based primarily on need.

You can read more about equity and equality in Chapter 3 and in Step 8 above.

Q2: 'When in Rome, do as the Romans do' – shouldn't organizations expect staff to conform to the organization's own norms and culture?

A: There is not a yes/no answer to this question. The norms and values of an organization are very important, but they should not be so inflexible that they do not allow deviation to cope with diversity. Local conditions may make it necessary to adopt a different approach. It is also important that the way something is done is the way it needs to be done and not just the way it has always been done - too many good ideas have been lost by a refusal to change for historical rather than real reasons.

You can read more about conforming to an organization's culture in Chapters 3, 6 and 8.

Q3: Can people not change and adapt their culture?

A: Yes they can, but it happens slowly. Much cultural change is generational rather than immediate. If people are required to change their culture, they need to know and accept the reasons. Managers also need to ensure that what they are asking does not conflict with the wider societal norms of a culture.

You can read more about cultural change in Chapter 5.

Q4: What is meant by diversity?

A: Diversity in the terms of this book is concerned with the management of people who may operate within a different culture or have different attributes to other members of the workforce. Diversity is a positive thing, it brings new ideas and experiences into an organization.

Q5: Does the glass ceiling really exist?

A: Unfortunately yes, but it is having less and less of an impact. Women still find that irrational barriers are placed in their way as they progress through both private and public organizations. The issue is one of considerable concern within society. Pragmatically, it means that much talent may be lost to an organization and that female staff may become demotivated as they see themselves barred from achieving their full potential.

You can read more about the glass ceiling in Chapters 6 and 8.

Q6: Wouldn't a team where the members are similar be more effective than a diverse set of personalities?

A: No, the work of Meredith Belbin has shown that diversity is a key component of team effectiveness. Teams need a balanced mix of members, not people who are similar.

You can read more about team roles in Chapters 1, 2, 3, 6, and 8.

Q7: How can modern technology assist the management of diversity?

A: Modern communications and information technology (ICT) can make it easier to find out about others and their way of life (and the reasons for it) and can also assist in the communications process across large distances.

You can read more about how modern technology can assist the management of diversity in Chapters 4 and 5.

Q8: Are the vast majority of people not motivated by the same things?

A: This was a central tenet of scientific management theory. People are, however, motivated by different things at different times in their lives. Money is not always the prime motivator. In some cultures, relationships and family may be just as important. Most people are more motivated by achievement and recognition as they progress through their careers.

You can read more about motivation in Chapters 1, 2, and 3.

Q9: What is the difference between prejudice and discrimination?

A: *Prejudice* is a set of beliefs held by an individual or group and based on the concept that others (either generally or specifically) are inferior to them, and therefore deserve to be treated less well. *Discrimination* is action against others in support of a prejudice and has been legislated against in many jurisdictions. Prejudice is thoughts and beliefs; discrimination is actions.

You can read more about prejudice and discrimination in Chapter 2.

Q10: What resources are available to assist in understanding the management of diversity?

A: Chapter 8 provides a list of the key concepts and thinkers on the management of diversity and Chapter 9 lists books, journals, software and web sites that will be of assistance.

Index

achievement   15, 80
achievement-oriented cultures   49
adaptation   103, 109
advertising   33
age diversity   55
alliances   66
allowable weaknesses   56, 106
Andreesen, Marc   22
anthropology   80
ascription   49, 80
asylum seekers   50-51
attitudes to time   46-7

behavior, psychological   6-7, 88
Belbin, Meredith   9, 18, 55-7, 67-8, 83-4
biodiversity   2
body language   23-4, 26-8, 51
bribery   47
British Airways, case study   65-70
bureaucracies   35, 43-4

case studies
   British Airways   65-70
   Coca-Cola   60-65
   Mitsubishi Heavy Industries   71-7
   Princess Cruises   37-9

caste   104
Certificate in Management Studies (CMS)   67
change, cultural   44-5, 110
Chenault, Ken   9
child labor   52
CMS *see* Certificate in Management Studies
Coca-Cola   60-65
collectivism   48, 50, 80
communications   12-13
   body language   23-4, 26-8, 51
   customer   106-7
   Internet   21-4
   remote   27-8
   video-conferencing   23-4, 27-8
   visual   86
companies, housing restrictions   14
concealed emotion   48
concepts   79-83
conflict, cultural   8, 80, 103-4
contingency management   17, 41, 42
contingency theory   80-81, 102
continuous professional development (CPD)   66
corporate identity   35

CPD *see* continuous professional development
Cross-Cultural Assessor software 87, 97–8
CRUISE program 37–9
culture
    analysis model 87
    change 44–5, 110
    definition 81
    global differences 32–3
    national trends 6–7, 40–45
    organizational 41, 42–4, 102–3, 105
customer care 37–9, 66–7
customers
    communications 106–7
    customer-centered products 72

Davidson, Marilyn J 84
DBT *see* design-and-build teams
dehumanization 22
demotivators 15–17, 21, 25, 110
design-and-build teams (DBT) 74–5
diffuse cultures 48–9, 81
DINKY, definition 81
disabilities 9–10, 55
discrimination 51, 57, 81, 107, 111
diversity 81

e-mail 22–4
early retirement 55
earnings gap 15, 90–91
economic refugees 50–51
emigration *see* migration
emotional culture 48, 81
empathy 32
entrepreneurial organizations 43–4
environment 7, 50
equity, equality comparison 11, 18, 20, 54, 106–7, 109
ethnicity 84, 88–9

ethnocentricity 5, 8, 10
evolution, human behavior 6–7, 88

family ties 34
financial motivation 15
FOS *see* Fundamentals of Supervision program
franchising 61, 62, 66, 68
frequently asked questions (FAQs) 109–11
Fundamentals of Supervision (FOS) program 66–70

gender 51–4, 86
    earnings gap 15, 90–91
    glass ceiling 52, 84, 88–9, 91, 110
ghettoization 17–18
glass ceilings 52, 84, 88–9, 91, 110
    definition 81
globalization
    communications 31
    cultural diversity 8
    definition 81
    empathy 32
    family ties 34
    Internet 29
    language 36
    legal issues 36–7
    religion 35–6
    social structure 34–5
    time differences 25–6
glossary 80–83
Gulliver software 88, 98

Hampden-Turner, Charles 90
Handy, Charles 44, 84–6
harmonic tension 2, 81
Harris and Morris 32
Harris, Philip 32, 86
Hastings, Colin 24
Herzberg, Frederick 15–17, 26
hierarchies 75

home working   24-5, 81
homogenous workforces   8-9, 10, 42, 81, 106
housing, company restrictions   14
hygiene factors   16-17, 82

identification, product   61
immigration *see* migration
imperialism   62
individualism   48, 50, 82
induction programs   43
industrial revolution   8
Internet   21-4, 29
Interplace software   83-4, 97
interpretation, advertising   33
investment, training   68
isolation   21, 25

job sharing   52-3

Kennedy, John F   2, 6
key aspects
   concepts   79-83
   frequently asked questions   109-11
   resources   93-9
   ten steps   101-7
   thinkers   83-91

language   7, 36, 83
   advertising   33
   communications   86, 106-7
   globalization   36
   variations   31
legislation
   disability   9-10
   discrimination   107, 111
   globalization   36-7
Lewis, Richard D   32, 86-8, 97-8
local loyalties   61-2, 65
Lynn, Matthew   71

matrix organizations   43-4
Mayo, Elton   15, 25
mergers   71
migration   9, 13, 19, 50-51
Mitsubishi Heavy Industries, case   71-7
Moran, Robert   32, 86
Morris, Desmond   26
motivators   82, 111
   financial   15
   recognition   16-17, 26
   selection   5
   self-sufficiency   55
mutiny   104, 195

national culture   45-50
nationalization   35, 65-6
neutral cultures   48, 65, 82
Nicholson, Nigel   7, 53, 80, 88

organizational culture   41, 42-4, 102-3, 105
over-achievement   15
overlap, cultural   8

part-time workers   52-3, 55
particularism   46, 47, 82
partnerships   43-4, 66, 72-7
Pendergrast, Mark   60
personalities   9, 82
personalization   26
Pettinger, Richard   20
politics   62, 65
popular culture   45
prejudice   5, 105
   definition   82
   discrimination   51, 57, 107, 111
   education   41, 57, 107
   gender   88-9
   inherited   8, 51
   language   83
primates   82

Princess Cruises, case study 37–9
privatization 35, 65–6
product identification 61
productivity 3, 55
psychological evolution 7
psychology 6–8, 80, 88
public transport 14
punctuality 46–7

racism 84, 88–9
refugees 50–51
religion 35–6, 103–4
resources 93–9
role theory 41, 55–7, 67–8

scientific management 9, 11, 14–15, 42, 82
sensitivity 105
slavery 13, 14–15
social animals 82
social structure 34–5
societal implications 85
software, suggested 97–8
specific cultures 48–9, 82
spending patterns 16–17
start-up costs 75
stereotyping 5, 7, 18
Stith, Anthony 88–9
sub-division development 14
suburban development 14
successes 59–77
suffrage 52
superteams 24
synergy 3, 18, 82, 106

Taylor, F W 9, 11
team building 83
team role theory 41, 55–7, 67–8, 82–4
technological changes 45, 54, 85
tele-cottages 25
thinkers 83–91
time, attitudes to 46–7
time differences 25–6
total quality management (TQM) 73
traditions 103–4
training
    FOS program 67
    global orientation 32–3
training providers 69
transport 12–14
Trompenaars, Fons 7–8, 32, 45–7, 89–90

universalism 46, 47
University of the Highlands and Islands (UHI) 27–8

video-conferencing 23–4, 27–8
visual communications 86

wage rates, global 106
weaknesses, allowable 56, 106
Wirth, Linda 90–91
workforces 60–70
    immigration 9, 13
    Japan 73